GASTRONATIVISM

ARTS AND TRADITIONS OF THE TABLE

**ARTS AND TRADITIONS OF THE TABLE
PERSPECTIVES ON CULINARY HISTORY**

Albert Sonnenfeld, Series Editor

■ ■ ■

For a complete list of titles, see page 227

GASTRONATIVISM

Food, Identity, Politics

FABIO PARASECOLI

Columbia University Press
New York

Columbia University Press
Publishers Since 1893
New York   Chichester, West Sussex
cup.columbia.edu
Copyright © 2022 Columbia University Press
All rights reserved

Library of Congress Cataloging-in-Publication Data

Names: Parasecoli, Fabio, author.
Title: Gastronativism : food, identity politics / Fabio Parasecoli.
Description: New York : Columbia University Press, [2022] | Series: Arts and traditions of the table : perspectives on culinary history | translated from Italian. | Includes bibliographical references and index.
Identifiers: LCCN 2021048860 (print) | LCCN 2021048861 (ebook) | ISBN 9780231202060 (hardback) | ISBN 9780231202077 (trade paperback) | ISBN 9780231554374 (ebook)
Subjects: LCSH: Food industry and trade—Social aspects. | Food—Political aspects. | Identity politics. | Nativism. | Food in popular culture. | Locavores.
Classification: LCC HD9000.6 .P373 2022 (print) | LCC HD9000.6 (ebook) | DDC 338.1/9—dc23/eng/20220104
LC record available at https://lccn.loc.gov/2021048860
LC ebook record available at https://lccn.loc.gov/2021048861

Cover design: Chang Jae Lee
Cover images: Shutterstock

CONTENTS

Preface vii
Acknowledgments xv

Introduction: Enter Gastronativism 1

PART 1: GASTRONATIVISM

1 Defending Privilege: Exclusionary Gastronativism 33
2 Toward a Better Future: Nonexclusionary Gastronativism 54

PART 2: THE POWER OF FOOD

3 Food and Identity 75
4 Food and Power 92

CONTENTS

PART 3: BORDERS AND FLOWS

5   Food, Nations, and Nationalism   111

6   Food and Diplomacy   126

7   National Products in the Global Market   140

PART 4: BETWEEN HERE AND THERE

8   Migrant Food   155

9   Contagions   172

Conclusion: What Future?   187

Notes   199
Index   223

PREFACE

IN MANY ways, this book has been in the making for a long time. I have been interested in international politics for many years: I studied it in college, I worked for a few years as a foreign affairs reporter, and even when I became a food writer, and then a food scholar, I continued to observe the political aspects of what we eat, how, and why. In my opinion, you cannot separate politics from food. We may enjoy reveling in memories and pastoral fantasies, celebrating flavors and traditions, and admiring the craft of chefs and artisans, but I believe there is more to food. Why has culinary nostalgia become so widespread? Why do we care about traditions? And why do chefs and artisans have plenty of customers who can understand and appreciate what they do, happy to pay a premium for it? These are profoundly political questions that I have been musing on for a long time in my research on the history and culture of food in Italy, popular culture, media, film, place-based labels, and food systems.

Such political questions have become more pressing. In recent years, I have watched countries where I live and do research (or have done research) fall into a spiral of a rabid populism, allowing the emergence of politicians that take advantage of widespread discontent to promote isolationism, conservatism, and various degrees of xenophobia. The United States, Italy, Poland, France, Brazil, China, India . . . all these places I have a connection with are now rife with conflicts and increasingly unsettled. Disgruntlement has turned into indignation and rage, and what and how people eat is often featured front and center in these dynamics.

Not for the first time, food plays a central role in politics, especially when not enough of it is produced or imported, or if people do not have enough to eat, for reasons ranging from natural disasters to social turmoil. While those concerns are still essential to most legitimate and illegitimate authorities at any scale, issues connected with individual and collective identities have taken center stage in ways that have turned food into a powerful ideological tool in political debates, protests, and negotiations. Food can be wielded as a weapon in cultural wars that, at times, become all too real, with devastating consequences for their victims. Moreover, while the apparent focus is on local or national issues, the horizon in which these tensions play out is more and more global.

Globalization appears to generate a need for community and rootedness that can be channeled into all kinds of political projects, operating at scales varying from the hyperlocal to the international. I have been looking for ways to make sense of these shifts both in my academic work and in other forms of communication, from books for general audiences to my own blog. In November 2019, I participated in the "Cucina Politica" conference at Bologna University. In Italian, the title means both political cuisine and political kitchen. Among the conversations that took place over the coffee breaks during the meeting, one stuck with me: some of the participants observed that the Italian left seems to have lost its capacity to relate effectively to politically charged ideas like nation or patriotism, which, in that country, have become the almost exclusive domain of right-wing and conservative discourse.

That exchange got me thinking, as it became apparent that the phenomenon was not limited to Italy. Why and how had that happened? Why are liberals and progressives less inclined to tackle those themes? Why can't the governments they head come up with effective yet humane and fair policies to manage migration flows, in order to prevent the rise of political forces that channel prejudice, racism, and xenophobia? Why don't enlightened intelligentsias seriously address concerns about the loss of cultural identity (even when it is mixed with racist and bigoted proclamations)? These matters cannot just be discounted, regardless of what we think of them or whether we consider them legitimate or based on facts. They exist and have tangible political implications. Liberal and progressive politicians appear to be aware of the consequences of the growing economic inequalities, both domestically and internationally, the transfer of blue-collar jobs to other countries, and the lowering of social status and standards of living among the middle and the working classes in high-income countries as well. However, their positions and declarations are often denounced as condescending and out of touch by those who bear the brunt of these epochal changes.

I am lucky enough not to share those same worries. I am part of the privileged, cosmopolitan, educated elite that populisms despise. I am an expert with credentials from prestigious institutions of higher education and I proudly strive to improve my expertise. I am an immigrant, although one of luxury, who relocated to a new country because of a cool job. I have all the traits of a globalist, to use a term very much *en vogue* in populist and nativist circles. I studied in different countries and traveled extensively as a journalist. Working in media, I witnessed the epochal transformation from local print and broadcast media to the present-day global circulation of news and images on the Internet. I still remember when we started talking about the Internet 2.0 and when I stopped using film to take pictures with an actual camera for my stories. Yet my personal path is not just that. I am not independently wealthy. My family, back in Italy, is neither powerful nor well connected. I guess I am among those who were able to ride the wave of globalization and make the most of it.

However, I am also well aware that many others did not have the same opportunities and were not able to access the same tools I mustered to advance my career. Some of them are among my friends and family. These reflections led me to read more about the contemporary politics of tribalism, populism, souverainism, nativism, nationalism, and all the other isms that are evoked to make sense of what we have been observing in the last couple of decades. I went back to classics of political thought, from Karl Polanyi to Hannah Arendt, but also started following right-wing media, although I must admit I could not force myself to read the most extreme publications for long. My goal was to get a better understanding of worldviews I deeply and viscerally disagree with. It was an intellectual endeavor as much as an existential one: taking a few steps back from current events to look at the big picture helped me maintain some sanity. I have always found writing therapeutic.

Each example I mention in the chapters that follow deserves deeper and more extensive exploration. The academic and general readership articles, as well as the books, throughout the endnotes, point to the importance of studies focusing on specific locations. I relied on sources in languages other than English to provide a variety of perspectives. I built on the wisdom of this material, together with my own research and reflection. However, I chose a different path, one that requires not only meticulous inquiry and observation but also the possibly reckless attempt at jumping high to embrace a bird's-eye perspective and detect patterns that would otherwise remain invisible on the ground. We know that maps are abstractions, but they are useful ones. They help us understand reality, taking us places we can then explore more closely. Different methods produce different maps, each with its own priorities and goals. No map gives us total knowledge, and we are aware we can get a variety of information by examining more than one map. In these pages I make a first attempt at a global map using food to detect possible patterns emerging from current events.

However, I am fully aware that these patterns are tentative, unstable, and shifting. They may disappear as soon as we recognize them, and there is no predetermined direction in which they are heading, since we shape them as we go: all is based on contingency and on the decisions of myriad actors. Anything can happen. For this reason, this book does not claim to have all the answers or, worse, to have found *the* answer to the current zeitgeist. Actually, it raises questions rather than offering solutions. However, it proposes one point of view, food and its ideological uses, to read events and tensions that are obviously much larger than what we eat or, rather, what the right stuff for us to eat is supposed to be. I turned to food not only because it is what I do for a living but also because food is an important aspect of the phenomena that are reshaping the global political landscape, although it is, at times, disregarded or treated with condescension. Food cultures and customs are not inconsequential ideological weapons. They have concrete impacts on the economic, legal, and social dimensions of our daily lives. For this reason, this book is not meant to be exclusively academic, although based on years of scholarly investigation and fieldwork. The topic is obvious and relevant to everybody, so I made my reflections as accessible as possible, with fewer endnotes than most scholarly works.

The past months have been extraordinary, and what happened, inevitably, has had an impact on my research and my writing. In early 2020, the pandemic upended our lives, forcing us into lockdown and changing the way we buy food or socialize around it. The summer of 2020 was marked by the Black Lives Matter protests, which put issues of systemic racism in the U.S. and elsewhere front and center, as the movement spread worldwide. At the same time, the food scarcity that whole populations have experienced during the pandemic has pointed to

PREFACE

inequalities in the global food system that politicians were leveraging in all kinds of ways. I was completing the first draft of this book when, on January 6, 2021, Trump supporters stormed Capitol Hill in Washington, D.C. They were not only right-wing extremists but also businesspeople, former soldiers, and policemen. The whole world watched, realizing how fragile the American political experiment is. The attack on the electoral process, fomented by the president himself, showed how shaky the foundations of democratic institutions are.

If anything, those events and incidents made writing this book even more urgent for me. The tense landscape of 2020 and 2021 has permeated all aspects of our social and personal life, food included. I hope that the following pages will help you look with fresh eyes at the ideological and political uses of food in the current state of affairs.

ACKNOWLEDGMENTS

I WANT to thank all those who have shared with me thoughts, fears, and doubts about politics and the political meaning of food. In particular, I am grateful to the organizers and the participants in the conferences "The Power of Taste" (Warsaw, Poland, October 2018), "L'alimentation comme patrimoine culturel" (Tours, France, November 2018), and "Cucina Politica" (Bologna, Italy, November 2019). The conversations that took place on those occasions have greatly influenced this book. My gratitude also goes to my students and colleagues at New York University and the other institutions where I have been invited to lecture or lead workshops, as well as to my coresearchers at the Institute of Philosophy and Sociology of the Polish Academy of Science in Warsaw: research is never an individual endeavor.

Of course, this work would have not been possible without the support of my friends and families, both in Italy and the

ACKNOWLEDGMENTS

U.S., despite the separations imposed by the pandemic. A special thank you goes to Doran Ricks, whose presence during the darkest moments of the lockdown kept me sane and grounded.

Thank you also to Esther Trakinski and Mateusz Halawa for their generosity in reading the first draft of the manuscript and providing precious feedback and to Maya Ruiz and Susan Pensak for editing my, at times, still wobbly English. I am grateful to Jennifer Crewe, Columbia University Press, and the anonymous peer reviewers for the opportunity to develop this project.

The research for this book has been partly made possible thanks to the startup fund provided to me by New York University, Steinhardt School of Culture, Education, and Human Development and by grant DEC-2017/27/B/HS2/01338 provided by the National Science Centre, Poland.

Arguments that led to this book had been previously explored or partially published in my blog fabioparasecoli.com; "Identity, Diversity, and Dialogue," in Darra Goldstein and Kathrin Merkle, eds., *Food: Identity and Diversity in Culinary Cultures of Europe* (Strasbourg: Council of Europe, 2005), 11–37; "Savoring Semiotics: Food in Intercultural Communication," in *Social Semiotics* 21, no. 5 (2011): 645–63; "Global Trade, Food Safety, and the Fear of Invisible Invaders," in *Social Research* 84, no. 2 (2017): 183–202; "Geographical Indications, Intellectual Property and the Global Market," in Sarah May, Katia Sidali, Achim Spiller, and Bernhard Tschofen, eds., *Taste Power Tradition. Geographical Indications as Cultural Property* (Göttingen: Universitätsverlag Göttingen, 2017), 13–24; "Eating Power: Food, Culture, and Politics," in Tomas Marttila, ed., *Discourse, Culture and Organization: Inquiries Into Relational Structures of*

ACKNOWLEDGMENTS

Power (Cham, Switzerland: Palgrave Macmillan, 2018), 129–53; "Tradition, Heritage, and Intellectual Property in the Global Food Market," in Ilaria Porciani, ed., *Food Heritage and Nationalism in Europe* (Abingdon: Routledge, 2019), 51–64; "The Invention of Authentic Italian Food: Narratives, Rhetoric, and Media," in Roberta Sassatelli, ed., *Italians and Food* (Basingstoke: Palgrave McMillan, 2019), 17–42; "The Power of Taste," in Jarosław Dumanowski, Andrzej Kuropatnicki, and Fabio Parasecoli, eds., *The Power of Taste: Europe at the Royal Table* (Warsaw: Muzeum Pałacu Króla Jana III w Wilanowie, 2020), 171–90; "Nativismi e contagi," in Massimo Montanari, ed., *Cucina politica: Il linguaggio del cibo fra pratiche sociali e rappresentazioni ideologiche* (Bari-Roma: Laterza, 2020), 175–89; "Super-market Forces," *MIT Technology Review*, January 2021, pp. 10–12.

GASTRONATIVISM

INTRODUCTION

ENTER GASTRONATIVISM

GRANTED, ITALIANS do tend to have strong opinions about their pasta and the traditions around it. However, when a pork-free lasagna was served at the Vatican in November 2019 during a charity meal for the poor, including several Muslim immigrants, the Italian political right freaked out. Building on their public discourse, which often reveals xenophobic undertones, they accused Pope Francis of being the bearer of a multiculturalist ideology that poses an existential threat to Christianity and Western civilization.[1] The elimination of pork from the dish was condemned as an attempt to make lasagna halal. So not Italian! This is just an episode that reveals the centrality of food and traditions—and their exploitation—in Italian political debates. In particular, its purity and authenticity stand out among the main sticking points. Disagreements about non-native elements in Italian cuisine are not new; they emerged together with the very idea of Italy as an independent country, following centuries

INTRODUCTION

in which the influence of foreign powers and their culinary customs—French, Spanish, Austrian, to name a few—helped shape Italian food as we know it.[2] However, in recent decades, the discussions have acquired a prominence in the public sphere and an acrimony in tones that set them apart from similar occurrences in the past. Why and how are they different? What historical, cultural, and economic developments have caused these changes? Who are their protagonists and what kind of ideas about society and politics do they embrace?

It is immediately evident that disputes ignited by alleged attacks against food traditions as symbols of cultural identity are not limited to Italy. The phenomenon is global, revealing common themes and attitudes in diverse contexts and across the political spectrum, from the most conservative to the most progressive positions. In turn, this raises the question of what circumstances may have brought about similar reactions around the world, all turning food into ideological fodder. In India, beef consumption has been used by fundamentalist Hindu movements, indirectly supported by the governing Bharatiya Janata Party (BJP) and Prime Minister Narendra Modi, as a motivation to organize attacks and lynching raids against Indians of Islamic faith, whose diet includes beef.[3] In 2017, the far-right and xenophobic political group Alternative für Deutschland (AfD, Alternative for Germany) transformed food into a Trojan horse for the defense of national identity and homegrown cultural traditions against migrants. The organization printed posters that read "Burka? I like burgundy wine better" or "Islam? It does not match our kitchen."[4] Also in Germany, following in the footsteps of Hitler's well-known vegetarianism, neo-Nazi groups have embraced veganism.⁵ They also make reference to themes such as organic farming, natural foods, and "clean" eating to connect with younger generations, while reaffirming the urgent need to defend the land and the national territory, echoing Nazi "blood and soil" motifs.⁶

The AfD was not the first contemporary European political movement to season food with ideology. In 2004, members of the Lega Nord party (since 2019 just Lega) served pounds and pounds of polenta, mixed with local cheese and butter, in a demonstration in the city of Como, Italy. Polenta, a porridge of ground maize flour, was served to passers-by to remind them of their roots and to underline the emotional and cultural value of a traditional dish that, in the past, was considered a quintessential staple of the poor. Posters reading "Yes to polenta, no to couscous" were plastered on walls, referring to the North African and Middle Eastern dish as shorthand for all immigrants. The slightest suspicion that local restaurants might add nonlocal ingredients to polenta became newsworthy.⁷ Similarly, in 2007 Nissa Rebela, a right-wing group in Nice, France, used the slogan "Yes to socca, no to kebab," identifying the socca, a local chickpea flour flatbread, as a symbol of resistance to immigration.⁸ These positions can generate policies. In the spring of 2009, the Tuscan city of Lucca passed regulations to ban all shops selling kebab, fast food, and other non-Italian fare from the historical quarter in the city center.⁹ The official rationale was the need to make sure tourists find those expressions of Italian cuisine that they have come to expect, regardless of the actual sociocultural transformation taking place all over the country.

INTRODUCTION

To be fair, turning to food to score political points is not exclusive to integralist or xenophobic movements. Sometimes, representatives of organizations for food producers adopt similar refrains and strategies to fight transnational corporations. In 1999 José Bové, a farmer activist and founder of the Confédération Paysanne (the Farmers' Confederation) of France, destroyed a McDonald's outlet under construction in Millau, Aveyron, to protest the penetration of the fast-food chain and the damage he argued it was inflicting on local rural economies and French culinary culture. The action was met with a certain sympathy in France, where the success of local agriculture has long been tied to the defense of local identities, often reflecting a culinary nationalism that sociologist Priscilla Parkhurst-Ferguson identified as a long-lasting phenomenon.[10] However, this time around, French debates were profoundly interwoven with and influenced by global dynamics connected with specific forms of contemporary trade and economic internationalization. In fact, moving away from the French context, Bové later became a spokesperson for La Via Campesina (the Farmers' Path), an international farmers' movement that originated in Latin America and promotes food sovereignty, the right for every community around the world to have a say in what they grow, what they consume, and what they import.

In these and other instances, food stands for a variety of forces ranging from migrants and internal countercultural agitators (often depicted as foreign agents or dupes of external enemies) to cosmopolitan globalists, financial elites, and transnational corporations, all bent on poisoning the minds and bodies of good people. Local, communal, ethnic, and traditional

INTRODUCTION

food practices become a catalyst for the resistance against external infiltrations and power grabs, wherever their source may be. The Lega Nord's refusal to consume couscous exudes nostalgia for a mythical past in which society was supposed to be simpler and less fragmented. Disdain for American-style fast food can express condemnation of globalization-driven uniformity. What is perceived as a foreign element is rejected as a possible cause for dilution or corruption of culinary identities and the culture in which they are rooted. When we look closer, we realize that debates about food are rarely just about food. In fact, looking at the world through the lens of food can help us better understand it.

FOOD BETWEEN DIPLOMACY AND TRADE WARS

How do these current manifestations of food as an ideological weapon differ from past manifestations of the use of food in politics and in general to exert power? It is certainly not the first time in history that food has acquired political meaning, ranging from the affirmation of class or ethnic privileges to the defense of cities, nations, and empires. This relevance is rooted in the material aspects of food systems and their historical manifestations. The production, importation, distribution, and availability of enough food to feed their subjects has been a constant concern for rulers and governments. The expansion of Rome from a small peripheral town in the Mediterranean to an empire was partly motivated by the need to secure wheat and

INTRODUCTION

other commodities for its growing population: at different times, Sicily, Northern Africa, the plains of Central and Eastern Europe all constituted sources for the nourishment necessary to the functioning of the Roman administrative and military machine. In seventh-century China, the Sui dynasty established a system of canals to facilitate the transportation of edible commodities between the South and the North, contributing to the reunification of the empire and its economic development after centuries of divisions and foreign invasions. Also in China, between the seventeenth and eighteenth century, the Qing dynasty organized a countrywide network of cereal warehousing and distribution. As rulers of foreign origin, it was particularly strategic for the Qing emperors to embody the ideal of the imperial sovereigns who took care of their subjects' well-being, both to gain the collaboration of bureaucrats and to avoid rebellions. Before their destruction at the hand of the Spanish conquistadores in the fifteenth century, the Incas built storehouses called *qullqua* to make food available to armies and conscripted laborers engaged in public construction projects. As food protests and riots can easily turn into revolutionary movements with larger political goals, prolonged hunger and unequal or unfair access to sustenance never bode well for the longevity of any kind of authority.

Because of its importance in the survival of governments, food often ends up expressing geopolitical tensions among nation-states. During the 2003 Iraq war, French fries became "freedom fries" for Americans who protested France's refusal to join the anti-Saddam coalition. It was not the first time that U.S. patriotism expressed itself through food. During World

War I, sauerkraut was at times referred to as "liberty cabbage," as anything coming from Germany was considered suspicious. This attitude, of course, caused problems for the German American community, one of the largest in the country at the time. In the same period, temperance and abstinence from drink were being promoted in the UK and Canada as forms of resistance against the barbarity of Prussia and Austria, represented as retrograde and repressive empires of drunkards. Rejections, boycotts, and protectionist measures against food products from other nations have been a mainstay in international relations.

For the same reason, food has been conspicuously featured in diplomatic activities, from official dinners to soft diplomacy efforts to promote national cuisines abroad. Decisions about what to serve during international events or high-level governmental meetings are influenced by the desire to showcase the best of each country's gastronomy and dazzle diners. Lavish abundance and culinary richness are meant to reflect economic wealth and political power. Moreover, countries frequently organize global campaigns to stimulate interest in their gastronomy and their products. Governments also intervene to defend their goods on the global market against counterfeits and to support their own food production.

FOOD AS IDEOLOGICAL TOOL

The way food is currently entangled with national and local debates, as well as certain commonalities of themes and approaches that can be observed around the world, points to something qualitatively different from what we have just discussed, often dubbed *culinary nationalism, gastronationalism,* or *gastrodiplomacy,* which tend to prioritize the nation as their strategic or ideological horizon.

As we will see in chapter 5, food plays an important role in nation-building and nationalism, and the attachment to nation-states is still significant in food-related debates and controversies.[11] Forms of food chauvinism have existed for as long as the nation has been a central organizing factor in social life. National allegiances are important, as refugees or people without their own country, Roma, Tibetans, Palestinians, or Rohingyas, can attest. However, nationality is not the sole discriminant determining what and how we eat. Our lives have become too complicated for that. We are witnessing phenomena that point to political positions and strategies that cannot be fully explained by nationality and nationalism only. The nation is just a factor, although a powerful one, among many that shape what we think and experience about our identity, while determining our sense of belonging.

Additional explanations are necessary to make sense of current developments. As individuals and communities find themselves operating at scales ranging from the local to the international, their preferences and decisions are the result of many overlapping and intersecting aspects of their identities, whether they are aware of it or not. The same person can make decisions and act according not only to their nationality and geographical location but also to their gender, class, education, occupation, origin, preferences as consumers, and travel

INTRODUCTION

experiences, just to mention a few. All these elements dynamically interact with each other, depending on the situation.

Building on these ever-shifting loyalties and identifications, social movements and political organizations turn to food to voice their discontent with their current circumstances or to imagine the future they desire. Once again, debates about food are not just about food. To describe these attitudes, strategies, and practices, I introduce the concept of *gastronativism*: the ideological use of food in politics to advance ideas about who belongs to a community (in any way it may be defined) and who doesn't.

The ideological use of food to establish political boundaries is not new. Plenty of historical precedents may be mentioned. As French philosopher Michel de Montaigne observed, "each man calls barbarism whatever is not his own practice."[12] Ancient Romans disparaged the foodways of the invading Germanic tribes as uncouth and disgusting, as they reflected a relationship with nature that was not based on agriculture and control of the environment but on hunting and gathering (or, at least, that was the Roman perception). The Chinese had an ambivalent relation with the eating habits of their Central Asian neighbors, and later with Mongolian and Manchu invaders. While they appreciated the fruits coming from today's Uzbekistan and from the oases around the Taklamakan Desert, and embraced tea with a vengeance, the Chinese considered their agricultural technology and their culinary practices vastly superior. The Spanish conquistadores could not recognize the way natives in the Americas cultivated their land as civilized agriculture. Accustomed to seeing tilled fields, where the traces of the plough were visible, they found it difficult to embrace the local methods, based on different approaches to land and water use. Furthermore, the newcomers introduced their own crops, such as wheat and grapes, and presented them to the local populations as symbols of a more advanced civilization. All Western imperialist powers in the nineteenth and twentieth centuries kept the foodways of the areas they colonized in very low esteem, all while appropriating them or exploiting them commercially.

Present-day gastronativism, however, differs from previous manifestations. It inevitably reflects not only the structure and flows of the global food system but also the social, economic, and political power relations that underpin it and determine its mechanisms. Food systems have been deeply impacted by the rapid and overwhelming changes connected to the specific processes of globalization that have emerged since the 1980s, particularly following the fall of the Berlin Wall. These transformations are closely connected with the neoliberal ideologies of the Washington Consensus and the economic policies that have emerged from it. More precisely, we can identify the root of contemporary gastronativism in the forms that globalization and the resistance against it have taken since the 2008 financial crisis, the long economic stagnation that ensued, and more recently, the COVID-19 pandemic.

The term *neoliberalism* has been criticized as all-encompassing and for that reason useless. It has certainly been evoked in ways that obscure its meaning, especially because it does not constitute a clear ideology explicitly embraced by politicians, parties, or social movements. In this book, *neoliberalism* refers to contemporary dynamics of globalization based on free trade, meant to

INTRODUCTION

achieve unrestricted flows of goods, people, ideas, money, and technology. Until recently, such arrangements flourished within a framework of multilateral international relations and organizations through a single logic of rule and a global form of sovereignty that Michael Hardt and Tony Negri described as *empire*, as opposed to imperialism based on national sovereignty.[13] The effects of neoliberal globalization as a political project are amplified by always faster and more pervasive technology and communication tools, from computer networks and big data to the Internet of Things and social media. At the national level, the role of governments has been downsized through deregulation, the privatization of public companies and services, and the weakening of welfare networks. The market is supposed to work at its best when left alone, allowing individuals and firms to express their preferences while providing the best guidance not only to maximize resources, but also to political management.

Against this background, local food systems all over the world have been integrated in ever-expanding networks, experiencing long-term structural changes brought about by technological innovation, industrialization, financialization, as well as the consolidation and expansion of transnational corporations. This state of affairs could be described as an emerging corporate "food regime."[14] The new rules of the game have brought about the delocalization of production and the transfer of jobs to locations where labor is less expensive. Inevitably, these transformations on the supply side end up influencing consumer choices at the supermarket, behaviors at the table, and discussions about the value and meaning of ingredients, dishes, and gastronomic traditions.

INTRODUCTION

WINNERS AND LOSERS

These epochal shifts have created winners and losers. While the global elites have profited from this state of affairs, a large part of the world's population has found itself excluded from the gains associated with neoliberal globalization.[15] Income inequality has increased, including in high-income countries.[16] Liberal democracy, which allows elected majorities to govern while protecting minorities and asserting the rule of law, has been increasingly attacked as a tool the elites use to keep the rest down. Swift technological advances and job offshoring damage those who do not have the capacity to adjust or to make a transition to other sectors, especially in the absence of public safety networks. The success of an economy is frequently measured by the performance of its stock market, to which only a tiny percentage of the population has access, or by its gross domestic product (GDP), which does not take into consideration the quality of life of citizens. Without any prospect of influencing or resisting globalization, whole areas of the world suffer from its consequences. The environmental impact is enormous and the social cost is stunning. Even in the richest countries, large segments of citizens are left without recourse, which generates resentment and grievances. The excluded and the victims, as well as those who fear their quality of life will worsen, resent those who have been able to take advantage of the changes thanks to their education, social relationships, or access to capital. Expanding unemployment, a sense of cultural loss, and the deterioration of social status have become common experiences for individuals and communities, which understandably feel threatened and overwhelmed by phenomena like climate change, mass migrations, terrorism, and pandemics. After all, these are just different facets of the same globalization processes.

The end of the Cold War has left a void in which capitalism and democracy have not won worldwide.[17] Old forms of tyranny and totalitarianism survive together with new authoritarian regimes that feed on populist and nationalist sentiments. As a consequence, no shared project for the political future of the international community has emerged, and the response is often a retreat to the local, the safe, and the parochial. The losers of globalization fear that their ways of life and their privileges can be even further reduced or taken away by those who are in even worse conditions than themselves. That includes not only the poor and the immigrant but also anybody who is different in terms of ethnicity, race, religion, sexuality, cultural identifications, social class, or political outlook. The result is that segments of the population that still hold significant power in a country may live in the constant anxiety of being erased or replaced, at times with vicious consequences. Such angst is easy to exploit politically.

Globalization is experienced in very tangible ways but operates through structures and dynamics so complex that they are difficult to fully understand. Experts, as well intentioned as they may be, are often deaf to the needs and priorities of ordinary people and unable to explain what happens in clear terms. They may end up talking down, rather than talking to, audiences who often feel demeaned and react by criticizing the elites as hypocrites that peddle virtues they do not practice themselves. The cosmopolitan

INTRODUCTION

elites, the globalists, and the highly educated can easily turn into representatives of mysterious and malicious powers that govern world events and technological transformations. Anybody with Internet access feels entitled to propose their own interpretations or to latch on and amplify the ones already circulating. Conspiracies spread widely, as they provide explanations that respond to fear, confusion, and disgruntlement.

Echo chambers in social media and social bubbles turn into parallel realities based on alternative facts that destroy the possibility to reach a consensus about anything and make people more susceptible to follow the solutions offered by populist leaders who forego any adherence to truth. Shrewd politicians can weave lies so enormous that there is no way to debunk them. Such "big lies," to reference historian Timothy Snyder's astute definition, thrive on emotional reactions, fidelity to the leader, and fanaticism that can easily turn from protest against the corruption of political and economic elites into violence and attempts at undermining the institutions of representative democracy.[18]

These tensions and the sense of constant crisis they generate favor the rise of heads of government that profit from them while stoking populism, nationalism, and isolationism: Jair Bolsonaro in Brazil, Rodrigo Duterte in the Philippines, Joko Widodo in Indonesia, Narendra Modi in India, Donald Trump in the U.S., Vladimir Putin in Russia, Jarosław Kaczyński in Poland, Viktor Orban in Hungary, and Recep Tayyip Erdoğan in Turkey are well-known examples. Such leaders do not need well-formed coherent ideologies: they simply activate a hodgepodge of ideas, instincts, emotions, values, and fears, speaking in ways that resonate with their supporters.[19] These

INTRODUCTION

politicians come across as direct (at times offensive), bold (often performing testosterone-laden masculinity), and bent on defending the "real" people from the elites to which, after all, they belong themselves.[20] Nigel Farage in the UK, Matteo Salvini in Italy, and Marine Le Pen in France have manage to channel discontent into powerful political movements that are increasingly interconnected and influential.

Not by chance, some of most infamous manifestations of gastronativism have appeared in the countries where these leaders operate. Food is able to activate emotions and does not require much mediation: everybody experiences it, everybody is an expert. In these contexts, gastronativism can achieve social and political results that go well beyond food. It interprets people's tangible experiences and frustrations as consequences of all-powerful, stealthy, and ruthless global dynamics, and it often does it through the language of victimization and sufferance. Gastronativism provides a sense of rootedness, comfort, and security against globalization. It counteracts the widespread sense that the world as we know it is breaking down. Saying no provides a sense of agency and empowerment. These tensions easily turn into contempt for the foods of the "others," who in different contexts can be transnational corporations, international organizations, stateless investors, cosmopolitan elites, immigrants, foreigners, ethnic minorities, religious communities, and other traitors who uphold principles of multiculturality and diversity. It is precisely the vagueness of the lurking enemy that turns gastronativism into an ever-shifting and adaptable political tool for politicians who know how to ride, and often stoke, discontent.

INTRODUCTION

LONGING FOR COMMUNITY

Intimate and psychologically powerful, food constitutes an arena to articulate anxieties deriving from contemporary life and linked to deep and complex socioeconomic shifts. Due to its role in anchoring individual and collective identities, it can be exploited to express all sorts of resentment and organize resistance.

As it contributes to establishing boundaries between "us" and "them," food can be implicitly political when it is not directly connected to any party or formal organization as well: it is a component of the life of the body politic, regardless of the scale at which it manifests itself, from a city to a region, a whole country, or the global scene. A community is a very specific kind of social grouping that can be based on identity factors as diverse as what is good and fair to eat, what is good for humans and the environment, where we come from, where we live, what we do, or who we hang out with. As political scientist Benedict Anderson has pointed out when examining the strength and efficacity of the idea of nation, communities can be imagined, establishing ties among individuals who may not actually interact among each other.[21] Thanks to technological developments in our means of communication, nowadays communities can be completely local or totally delocalized. The same peasant community in Nicaragua may have a strong sense of its local identity, while being aware of belonging to the transnational peasant movement. It can organize a protest against local representatives of the government while planning strategies with other communities sharing similar priorities or situations in Sudan or Indonesia.

INTRODUCTION

Whatever their connective tissue may be, communities are central to gastronativism, even when not always explicitly expressed or addressed. A sense of bonding among its members seems necessary for gastronativist positions to emerge. Such strong and, at times, emotionally charged ties do not always need to be explained or justified, because they are supposed to be experienced as gut feelings, without mediation.[22] They establish a profound sense of communal identity that then is projected onto the rest of society to assess its past, negotiate its present, and imagine its future.

We sometimes define the "Others," the people we experience as different and potentially threatening, based on how their food customs reflect their spiritual beliefs: Muslims identify nonbelievers through their consumption of pork, alcohol, and nonhalal products. Orthodox Jews may feel uncomfortable sitting at a table where the dietary rules of kashrut are not followed, including when eating with more secular members of the Jewish community. Indians from Brahmin castes tend to avoid sharing meals with people of other castes, but are often more flexible when they find themselves living in new locations, both within the country and abroad. Contrasts among generations can activate a sense of "us" and "them" regardless of nationality, religion, or education. Middle-aged people occasionally make fun of avocado toast and natural wines, using them as shorthand for hipsters and the shortcomings ascribed to them, often with class undertones. Rifts appear within the same national community, even within the same city, along the lines of cultural wars.

Concurrently, correspondences and solidarities can manifest across countries. In terms of values, attitudes, and eating habits, urban, educated, and upwardly mobile cosmopolitan foodies may have more to share with their peers in other parts of the world than with neighbors who may have different levels of education, socioeconomic status, and exposure to social media. Even when trying to recruit them, antiglobalization activists may look with disdain on those who patronize fast-food restaurants or have no objections against consuming food containing GMO ingredients, regardless of nationality. A smallholder farmer understands the experiences and problems of other farmers, wherever they are located; the expansion of La Via Campesina peasant movement and the success of Terra Madre, the meeting of farmers organized every two years by the international association Slow Food, are cases in point.

FOOD DEBATES ARE NEVER JUST ABOUT FOOD

Gastronativism has developed into a worldwide phenomenon that operates through multifaceted global interconnections. Its themes, attitudes, and strategies often display striking similarities across distant, and apparently unrelated, geographical and cultural contexts, revealing unexpected yet meaningful associations. Moreover, their protagonists may establish—at times accidentally, at times intentionally—recurrent dialogues or more long-term, formalized collaborations.

For this reason, it is necessary to take the risk of conducting an expansive investigation: having its origin in globalization, gastronativism can only be examined by thinking globally.

INTRODUCTION

Trying to connect dots and identifying common threads, however, is an uncertain endeavor, because it is easy to fall into generalities that do not clarify anything. It is also a difficult one, as making sense of gastronativist ferments requires tackling fields as diverse as culture, media, political theory, international affairs, economics, and trade. In other words, it is best to embrace an interdisciplinary approach, one that can tackle food in all its complexity. I have responded to this challenge by building on food studies, a field of research and practice that looks at food as a "total social fact," a category described by anthropologist Marcel Mauss as phenomena that "are at once legal, economic, religious, aesthetic, morphological and so on. . . . They are at once political and domestic, being of interest both to classes and to clans and families."[23] Food studies analyzes biological, cultural, social, economic, technical, and political issues concerning the production, distribution and consumption of food in its material and immaterial aspects.[24] Jeff Miller and Jonathan Deutsch define it as "not the study of food itself but rather the study of the relationships between food and the human experience. These relationships are examined from a variety of perspectives and from a range of places in the food system, from production to consumption, or from 'farm to fork.'"[25] As a consequence, "food studies research runs a broad gamut of topics, home disciplines, theoretical orientations, and research methodologies. . . . Such diversity makes food studies compelling and opportunities numerous."[26] As we already discussed, political controversies about food are rarely about food; looking at them through the lens of food generally and gastronativism specifically, we can better understand them. For this reason, food studies proves to be an appropriate tool to assess what is behind gastronativism and its impact on contemporary politics.

Food studies offers in-depth reflections about many of the key concepts that constitute the toolkit of this book: identity, tradition, authenticity, community, and memory, among others. As it looks at food as a total social fact, food studies also provides the opportunity to observe materiality, discourse, practices, and institutions both in their specificities and in their interconnections, overcoming disciplinary distinctions between agency and culture on the one hand and structure and systems on the other. The lasagna without pork we discussed at the beginning of this introduction is, at the same time, an object with specific textures and flavors, a dish that can be judged in terms of taste, recipe, tradition, and authenticity, an element in a specific event and in the protests that followed it, and the expression of institutional objectives that ended up clashing with the goals of other political movements, organizations, and institutions. For this reason, food studies allows us to look at food in all its political complexity, without artificially separating the spheres of social life in which it appears and operates through behaviors, words, and imagination.[27] Using its tools, we can examine what individuals and communities say, make, and do around food to push ahead their agendas about what society is and should be.

GASTRONATIVISM AND ITS MANIFESTATIONS

Neoliberal globalization and the often profound—and relatively sudden—transformations that it has imposed on large swaths

INTRODUCTION

of humanity has generated a wide array of responses. In its embrace of food as identity anchorage and ideological tool, gastronativism reflects a variety of political positions and reactions ranging from defense of local agrobiodiversity to distrust of foreign and unfamiliar products, at times with isolationist or xenophobic undertones. Its protagonists often adopt bottom-up, grassroots strategies, regardless of their political goals, displaying a gamut of attitudes from the staunchest conservatism to the most iconoclastic progressivism: the impact of their manifestations depends on the political projects they become part of.

Gastronativism tends to be exclusionary when it is based on the tangible and emotionally charged defense of the status quo against internal and external forces, trying to limit access to the perceived privileges that come with belonging to a community. White supremacy in the U.S., anti-immigrant movements in Italy, conservative identity politics in Poland, and Hindu hegemonic efforts in India find enemies not only outside of the country but also inside. Often conservative or reactionary, these movements invoke democracy as the unfettered rule of the majority (or what is presented as an often imaginary "silent" majority), forfeiting the liberal niceties about the protection of minorities and the rule of law. For this reason, exclusionary approaches are easily co-opted in authoritarian and autocratic projects that erode democratic norms and institutions. Within this framework, food often embodies the desire for a mythical, often imagined past when things were as they should be. When it plays within national borders, exclusionary gastronativism aims to achieve social class, race, and ethnic distinctions, identifying true and worthy culinary traditions, free of impurities and miscegenation. It tends to defend patriarchy, underlying the role of women in food preparation and sanctifying the family meal. It puts religions and their moral principles back at the center of social life, paradoxically often ignoring kindness, charity, or spirituality: the defense of Christian foodways can be upheld as a lofty goal, all while ignoring the Gospel's invitations to feed the poor and the hungry. Gastronativism supports the hegemony of common sense and mainstream attitudes against any kind of counterculture, from veganism to dumpster diving. It favors a sense of unity among the "real people" who recognize themselves as part of the same community, without the mediation of governments, institutions, or intellectuals.

However, not all forms of gastronativism strive for exclusion. Some aim instead toward extending rights, resources, and well-being to the disenfranchised and the oppressed. I recognize three distinct currents within nonexclusionary gastronativism, which—just like the exclusionary ones—are a reaction against neoliberal globalization and its representatives, which turn into the catalysts for their emergence and the targets of their strategies. As the issues they deal with are felt worldwide, the nation is not their sole horizon of action. These movements aim at creating diffused communities that deal with similar struggles across borders, regardless of nationality, ethnicity, race, gender, and (in some cases) class.

The first current of nonexclusionary gastronativism consists of the antiglobalization movements that identify their enemies with transnational corporations, their exploitative supply chains,

INTRODUCTION

their environmental impact (from water pollution to deforestation), and their recourse to intellectual property to appropriate genetic material, traditional practices, and indigenous knowledge. These movements try to defend "us" as consumers and citizens against big business and the political and economic structures that support it. To do so, they invoke radical, structural changes and manifest antiauthoritarian or anarchical streaks.

At times, this current partly overlaps with a second current of nonexclusionary gastronativism, which can be identified with elements within the so-called food movement. Increasingly vocal and organized in the Global North, it imagines more just and inclusive food relations based on citizens' participation. Opposing the homogenization that comes with globalization, this current usually expresses a preference for reforming the existing food system rather than revolutionizing it, despite the rhetoric it may employ. When it reflects the priorities of the most affluent segments of the population, these attitudes can easily turn into forms of elitism that ignore or discount the needs and values of those who are considered less enlightened and in need of guidance and education.

The third current of nonexclusionary gastronativism is the food sovereignty movement. In this case, minorities or disadvantaged sectors of the population (mostly farmers, often belonging to racially or ethnically marginalized communities located in developing countries) demand equality and self-determination. The "other" against which these movements emerge can be local and national politicians, international organizations, and transnational corporations. Their mode of intervention can be confrontational, launching political initiatives directed at changing the underlying structures in the food system.

To examine these different forms of resistance to neoliberal globalization, this book is organized in four parts. Part 1 explores the exclusionary and nonexclusionary forms of gastronativism. Part 2 examines why food finds itself at the core of gastronativist attitudes: the focus is on the political meaning of food, and on food as an expression of identity through ideas and practices of tradition, authenticity, and heritage. Part 3 looks at the role of nation, nationality, and nationalism in international relations, diplomacy, and trade. This part also assesses how nation-focused politics interact—and at times clash—with the disruptive and shifting objectives, ideals, and strategies of gastronativism, which emerge and operate on a global horizon. Part 4 analyzes the relationship between food and migrants, one of the hot-button gastronativist issues that politicians often exploit to get knee-jerk reactions from voters. This part also reflects on the metaphors of invasion and contagion, which have often been used to describe migrants and their food and culinary practices, becoming painfully visible during the COVID-19 pandemic.

AND NOW, A QUICK DETOUR INTO POLITICS

By now, the political nature of gastronativism should be evident. However, if you are mostly interested in food issues, you can skip this quick detour into politics and move to the next chapter. If you instead want to get more background information about the topics we are exploring, bear with me for a few more paragraphs.

I developed the concept of gastronativism by expanding on the analytical framework developed to assess the values, goals, and strategies of nativism, a recurrent and evolving political attitude in U.S. history. Historian John Hingham outlined it as "intense opposition to an internal minority on the grounds of its foreign (i.e., 'un-American') connections."[28] His definition leaves open the question of foreignness, which can also be attributed to segments of the domestic population. Not for nothing, in recent times attempts at addressing structural racism or at establishing a public healthcare system have been dubbed "un-American," even when originating from within the U.S. For political scientists Benjamin Knoll and Jordan Shewmaker, nativism is the "individual-level attitude that a unique American culture and way of life needs to be protected against foreign influence."[29] The main point is the sense that one's culture (whatever that may be at different points in time) is like nobody else's, and it is threatened. Legal scholar Lindsay Huber and colleagues described nativism as "the practice of assigning values to real or imagined differences, in order to justify the superiority of the native to the benefit of the native and at the expense of the non-native, thereby defending the native's right to dominance."[30] However, the notion of who counts as a "real" native is at least blurred. Although nationality and citizenship are still central to these debates, they are not the sole factor determining which individuals and communities can claim to represent the "true" essence of a nation.

INTRODUCTION

Nativism first emerged in the 1850s in U.S. movements such as the Know Nothing Party that opposed the immigration of Catholics from Ireland and Germany, perceived as a menace by local Protestants. From the beginning, this political attitude was fluctuating and hard to pinpoint, as Protestants themselves were either immigrants or descendants of immigrants. Nativism resurfaced at the end of the nineteenth century against Jewish and Southern European newcomers after World War I as a reaction to the Red Scare embodied by anarchic immigrants, local labor organizers, and leftist intellectuals, as well as during the Great Depression. Often the descendants of those who had been nativism's victims embraced nativist attitudes toward new waves of immigrants. Nowadays, as historian Peter Schrag has observed, the "immigrant's face" is put on "inchoate economic and social anxieties—the flight of jobs overseas, the crisis in health care, the tightening housing market, the growing income gaps between the very rich and the middle class, and the shrinking return from rising productivity to labor."[31]

I chose to expand on the American experience of nativism because the United States has been intertwined, since its founding, with globalization and the swift transformations it entails. The country's economic expansion and its political power have been connected with globalizing dynamics, even during the periods in which the country seems to close up on itself. In some ways, the causes of the different waves of American nativism seem to parallel those of current gastronativism. Established by immigrants, whom the indigenous natives experienced as dangerous "others," the United States has alternatingly welcomed and despised immigrants, who have nevertheless contributed to its expansion. It was precisely economic growth that required more labor than was available and that had to be found elsewhere.

Today's nativist reactions outside the U.S. are also unleashed by the arrival of migrants, who often practice a different religion from the majority. In Italy, Hungary, and Poland, the defense of Western culture and Christian civilization is often invoked to limit foreign—read Muslim—immigration, all while welcoming investments from the Muslim world. Muslim countries, in turn, tend to favor Muslim immigrant workers regardless of their provenance and ethnicity: the Muslim community of Kerala, for instance, has profited from the welcome its members receive in the Gulf emirates. That does not exclude droves of Catholic Filipinos from being employed, though . . .

Nativist contempt has been variously justified by and based on factors that go beyond nationality and religion and include race, culture, and education. At times, nativism is focused against internal immigrants. Any kind of difference can be condemned as the expression of "ideologies," such as LGBTQ, multiculturalism, relativism, or political correctness. Alert cries are sounded against the penetration of corrupting cultural approaches into education such as critical race theory and gender theory. This allows nativist attitudes to develop against extraneous elements in what is supposed to be the "real" body politic. In fact, not only groups of people but also ideas, goods, technology, and information can be perceived as non-native.

Nativism periodically expands during periods of fast social and economic transformations that shake the citizens' sense of security, often in connection with urban expansion, demographic changes, and vast population movements. Similarly, today's gastronativism is a reaction to growing inequalities and mass migrations, with the difference that it now has global social media at its disposal to shape its discourse and its practices. Responding to the ever-present question of who is fit to be included in the national project, the identity of who counts as "us" and as "them" has varied enormously.

Despite its specific origins in the U.S., I chose to use nativism as the template for gastronativism, because since its inception it has always been shiftier in its goals, more varied in its motives, and more flexible in its manifestations than other political attitudes that could legitimately be used as a lens to explore the ideological uses of food. Moreover, the reference to nativism, rather than to categories like populism, souverainism, nationalism, and other forms of imagined communities, underlines the inherent entanglement of the phenomenon with globalization, although it may find expression at the local, regional, or national levels.

Nativism differs from European souverainism (*souverainisme* in French, *sovranismo* in Italian, *soberanismo* in Spanish), a reaction against multilateralism, the rule of treaties, and the authority of international organizations, above all the European Union and its impersonal and nonelected bureaucracy, which is experienced as imposing oppressive rules and standards. The goal of souverainism is for every single nation-state to possess the ultimate say over its own decisions through the exercise of full sovereignty. Nativism does not totally overlap with populism either, which emphasizes less the aspect of community and its boundaries than the fight of ordinary people against corrupted elites, established power structures, and the professionalization of politics, which are all deemed expression of liberal democracy and its "political correctness." Nativism also diverges from patriotism, which expresses loyalty and love for one's nation to the point of sacrifice, and nationalism, which prioritizes the defense of the nation-state's interests and the appreciation of its culture above all others.

To summarize, American nativism, although imbued in nationalistic spirit, offers a template to understand contemporary forms of gastronativism in that it is constantly evolving and always responding to rapid transformations in its surroundings, felt as threats connected with globalization and internationalization. It is based on negotiations about who belongs and who doesn't, at times emphasizing foreignness, at times differences and tensions within the community itself; finally, it can be coopted in all kinds of projects along a spectrum that spans from rabid conservatism to semirevolutionary progressivism. Having clarified the meaning of gastronativism as a tool to examine political movements that use food as an ideological weapon, we can now move on and look closer at different kinds of aspects of the phenomenon.

PART ONE

GASTRONATIVISM

Chapter One

DEFENDING PRIVILEGE

EXCLUSIONARY GASTRONATIVISM

IN JUNE 2019, a video went viral across the Islamic world, supposedly filmed in Bareilly, Uttar Pradesh, India.[1] In it, four construction workers are harassed and beaten by a group of men for eating beef. The workers try to explain they were eating buffalo, but it was not enough to stop the attackers. Unfortunately, this is not an isolated incident. The chief minister of Uttar Pradesh, Yogi Aditynath, a Hindu monk and a representative of the Hindu fundamentalist Bharatiya Janata Party (BJP), banned cow smuggling after his election in 2017 and has been extremely vocal against illegal slaughterhouses. The consumption of beef has become an intense point of dispute between those who believe that India should be a Hindu nation and those who instead support liberty of religion and the rights of all minorities, turning eating beef in public into a form of political protest.[2] This episode is just a manifestation of long-lasting strains dating back to the partition of British India into two independent countries, India and Pakistan, in 1947. The mistreatment of Muslim citizens in India and the lack of respect for their dietary customs and rules have had enormous resonance throughout the Islamic world.

Food was again at the center of interreligious strife—this time with nationalistic undertones—when in 2020 a French teacher was beheaded for showing a caricature of the prophet Muhammad in class. French president Emmanuel Macron reacted by vowing to stop Islamic fundamentalism from subverting the French ideals of a secular nation and by asking French Muslims to explicitly adhere to republican ideals. It was the last episode of the enduring reckoning of France with its imperial history and the massive presence of immigrants from former colonies, many of whom are Muslims. The terrorist attacks by Islamic fundamentalists, especially the massive ones in Paris in November 2015 and on July 14, 2016, have given new fuel to existing debates about women's (especially young girls') use of the headscarves in school and in public spaces, and the tensions between halal rules and EU-issued regulations about animal slaughtering. As demonstrations against fundamentalist violence multiplied in France after the 2020 beheading, Muslim-majority countries around the world called for a boycott of its products. Turkish prime minister Recep Tayyip Erdoğan invited his countrymen to stop buying French goods, while street protests took place in Bangladesh and calls to boycott stores of the French supermarket chain Carrefour were heard in Saudi Arabia and Kuwait.[3] The long-term consequences of such campaigns, however, have been limited, as some Middle

Eastern countries import wheat from France, a main staple for their populations.

Religion intersects not only with nationality but also with sexual orientation to constitute a motivation for gastronativist incidents. In the summer of 2020, Palestinian Islamic religious leaders called for the boycott of Al Arz Tahini, a brand of hummus produced by an Israeli Arab company that had provided funding for a hotline for LGBTQ Arabs.[4] Grocery stores and supermarkets stopped selling the product, while supporters of the initiative asked consumers to buy more of it. The controversy highlighted the fault lines among Arab Muslims regarding who really counts as a member of the community and who needs to be isolated as a threat to its spiritual and social well-being.

A ZERO-SUM GAME

These examples of gastronativism, as diverse as they may appear, all reflect an exclusionary mindset: the defense of one's community against both internal and external perceived menaces requires the condemnation and at times the legal, physical, or metaphorical exclusion of those who do not belong. No need to think too much about who is part of the "real" community: its members are supposed to intuitively know it. They recognize each other, among other things, by what they eat—how and with whom—and what they produce and buy. Those who subscribe to this worldview experience politics as a zero-sum game: whenever one gains, somebody else loses. Those who make demands that could potentially chip away at the way of life, the prerogatives, or the privileges of a community, automatically become its enemies. It does not matter if these foes are weaker and more vulnerable than the members of the "in" group, or if they are just demanding the recognition and respect of their rights as citizens. The social and political arrangements that could derive from embracing the positions of those who live or act according to outlooks that do not coincide with the "real" community are branded as "wrong," "sacrilegious," "unnatural," "abnormal," or just plain "weird."

Cannibalism is the ultimate accusation that can be leveled at a community that is experienced as so totally foreign as to be dangerous. During the Middle Ages and all through the Counter-Reformation, Jews were accused of eating Christian children in ritual murders or adding their blood to Passover matzah, a theme that has become a staple of anti-Semitic propaganda.[5] The indigenous populations of the Caribbean were demeaned in the eyes of the European colonizers by allegations of anthropophagy, an issue that is still the object of scholarly debates.[6] The slogan "Communists eat children" became a catchphrase in the political polemics that raged in Italy after World War II, when the anti-Communist propaganda of the pro-U.S. Christian Democracy Party, often amplified by the Sunday sermons of local priests, was fighting the influence of the Italian Communist Party, accused of acting under the authority of the Soviet Union.[7] The urban myth probably emerged from rumors connected with the extremes of the famines that devastated Russia and the Ukraine after the October

Revolution and with supposed acts of cannibalism during the siege of Leningrad in 1941.

When it is the focus of exclusionary gastronativism, food can become a symbol of national sovereignty, cultural purity, or social unity, depending on the context. The three dimensions sometimes overlap. Local tensions can be variously read as expressions of a long list of far-reaching, often intersecting epochal clashes: civilizations vs. savagery, democracy vs. totalitarianism, national sovereignty vs. global world order, progressive vs. conservative worldviews, science vs. opinion, innovation vs. tradition, western Christianity vs. Islam vs. Judaism, Hinduism vs Islam, and so on. Gastronativism easily finds justification and legitimacy in these overarching narratives.

Space and geography can provide effective points of reference to stoke resentment and boost the sense of "us" against "them" that gastronativism thrives on. It is easy for politicians and political movements to promote their ideological agendas by leveraging the emotional attachment and sense of pride in culinary traditions of localities at various scales: a country, a region, or even a city. Nation and nationality can constitute the horizon for gastronativist ideas and actions to emerge, but they are far from being the only one. The point of contention may be imports from other countries or the crops and food customs from another region within the same country. Foodways and dishes of a city or even a specific neighborhood can be disparaged as decadent, harmful, or coarse. Space lends itself well to the establishment of boundaries, which constitute powerful engines in gastronativism as they are meant to separate communities, totally ignoring their concurrent function as points of contact for exchange and communication.

Although tensions frequently surface with geographical frontiers as their more immediate focus, their actual horizon is global, as these attitudes tend to emerge in reaction to worldwide and seemingly unstoppable phenomena such as transnational business, international trade, mass migrations, and climate change. Moreover, the simplification of diverse and complex food meanings into a single, easily digestible point of view is favored by the borderless circulation of information, ideas, and political attitudes. The populist and souverainist Italian Lega we encountered in the introduction can connect and find legitimacy for its political strategies in similar movements elsewhere, from the right-wing xenophobia growing in Western Europe and the resistance in Eastern Europe to progressive ideas that are marked as foreign and dangerous, to the America First attitudes of Donald Trump's followers, Hindu fundamentalism in India, and white supremacist proclamations by Jair Bolsonaro in Brazil. Through food, these forces conflate geographical boundaries with cultural, ethnic, and religious differences. While the Lega upheld polenta as a unifying symbol, the others have respectively emphasized pork products, rosół Sunday broth, fast food, vegetarianism, or culinary traditions rooted in European origins as their call to arms. The choice of food may depend on the context, but the dynamics that turn it into an ideological weapon are similar.

The tensions between Palestinians and Israelis that have grown around the foraging of wild herbs in the Occupied Territories offer a good case in point. Za'atar (*Majorana syriaca*) and 'akkoub (*Gundelia toumerfortii*) have traditionally played an important role in Palestinian cuisine, together with fennel, dandelion, and wild asparagus. In spring, it is possible to make whole meals out of these plants, with the simple addition of salt, olive oil, and grains.[8] However, the Israeli government declared za'atar and 'akkoub "protected plants," respectively in 1977 and 2005, as part of a larger effort to safeguard biodiversity. Legitimate scientific concerns about sustainability and overharvesting are enmeshed in claims about civilization and culture. The new regulations inevitably clash with Palestinian long-standing practices that can be incriminated not only for foraging what they experience as everyday components of their diet but also for possessing or trying to sell them.[9] The Israeli Nature Protection Laws have criminalized Palestinian herb-picking culture, which in turn Palestinians have embraced as an act of resistance against the perceived encroachment of Israelis on land they consider theirs.

Disputes about herbs are part of much longer confrontations about the use of soil and water that started with the first Zionist settlements in the late nineteenth century and continue today. Such conflicts have constituted flash points in international politics and global trade. In recent years, a movement has emerged to boycott, divest, and sanction Israeli products, including food. To counter this form of protest in the U.S., and in a final attempt to support the policies established by Israeli prime minister Benjamin Nethaniahu, former president Donald Trump's secretary of state, Mike Pompeo, announced that products from Israeli settlements in the West Bank would be imported into the U.S. with a "Made in Israel" label, making it more difficult to distinguish them from other Israeli products. In an attempt to squeeze the thorny politics around Israel and the Occupied Territories into one crude ideological tool, the Trump administration tried to label every attempt at protesting Israeli settlements in the West Bank as antisemitic. In a show of solidarity, Pompeo visited the Psagot Winery, built on what was previously privately owned Palestinian land.[10] The company, incidentally, is owned by the Florida-based Falic family, which apparently financed both Trump's and Netanyahu's reelection campaigns.[11]

Disputes about the use of land for food production turn into broad assertions about culture and civilization as well in the treatment that nomadic or seminomadic pastoralists communities have frequently received from the media in countries where national authorities try to force them to "modernize" or renounce their customs. Their lack of respect for borders, both territorial and symbolic, can provoke gastronativist backlash regardless of nationality and religion. Sedentarism would allow governments to better control pastoralists politically and to make them an easier target for taxation and other regulations. In countries like Kenya, China, and India, pastoralists have been described as vulnerable, lacking business acumen, and damaging to the environment.[12] Their production methods are depicted as backward and unhygienic, their products unsafe. However, pastoralist methods, refined over generations in often harsh environments, allow for an efficient use of water and pasture, offer resilience against climate change, and can enhance food security for entire communities. In Ethiopia, the government has targeted herders in semiarid lowlands, ostensibly in an attempt to "decolonize" them and support their economic development, while international NGOs and public opinion have framed them as marginalized communities that are particularly exposed to droughts.[13] As climate change worsens tensions around the use of resources, pastoralists get caught in struggles among themselves and with sedentary farmers, often along ethnic lines.[14] Conflicts are intensified because of the absence of property rights or, rather, because of conflicting approaches and customs about ownership between pastoralists and the government.[15] The introduction of ethnic-based federalism, which was supposed to better reflect the complex composition of the Ethiopian population and deal with long-standing inequalities among different groups,[16] has not eased the disagreements.

OF BEEF AND OTHER MEATS

The ideological use of food to exclude whole communities from full citizenship is particularly complicated in India, where regional differences overlap with religion, class, and caste tensions. The consequences in terms of activist campaigns and even governmental policies have been nefarious, variously described as "culinary apartheid,"[17] "dietary profiling," and "food fascism."[18]

Candidates for the BJP in India and supporters of political movements inspired to Hindutva, a form of Hindu nativism popularized by Vinayak Damodar Savarkar in the 1920s, are to various degrees favorable to the nationwide imposition of Hindu dietary requirements such as the rejection of meat, beef in particular. Hindu fundamentalists often impute the introduction of carnivorous behaviors to the Mughal, a Muslim dynasty from Central Asia that in the sixteenth century occupied most of Northern India (where Muslim sultanates actually already existed). By so doing, they contribute to marking Muslim communities as "other," turning them into potential targets for violence.

Cow protection vigilante groups, known as *gau rakshak*, have attacked and at times murdered individuals accused of bringing cows to slaughter, which is illegal in states such as Gujarat, Punjab, and Rajasthan, even when they were actually transporting dairy cows with official permits. The BJP's ideological powerhouse, Rashtriya Swayamsevak Sangh (the National Volunteers' Organization), pushed for a national ban on cow slaughtering, meant to "prevent uncontrolled and unregulated animal trade" in livestock markets. However, the ban was suspended by India's Supreme Court.[19] Such measures are widely perceived as a threat against the Indian buffalo industry, which exports meat in large quantities to countries like Indonesia, Malaysia, and Egypt. The Agricultural and Processed Food Products Export Development Authority of India (APEDA), projected that over three billion dollars' worth of buffalo meat was exported in 2019–20.[20] Leather production would also have been heavily damaged.

By reverting to vegetarianism, Hindu fundamentalists aim to symbolically regain an original state of purity found in ancient traditions. Needless to say, such interpretation of Indian history and its political instrumentalization are resisted by those who oppose the forceful imposition of Hindu beliefs on the rest of the population and by scholars that point to how Indian rulers (including Hindu ones) had actually consumed all kinds of meat at different points of history. *Kshatriyas*, the caste historically connected with war and defense, routinely ate meat (and drank alcohol), differentiating themselves from the Brahmin upper castes. Historians have hypothesized that Brahmins embraced meat avoidance in order to distance themselves from animal sacrifices that, in antiquity, had played a central role in religious rituals, as Buddhist and Jain notables were also vegetarian.

B. R. Ambedkar, an activist for the untouchable, or *dalit*, caste and an architect of the Indian constitution, argued that food distributes Hindus into three large groups with very different access to power: at the top of the social hierarchy those who avoid flesh, in a median position those who consume nonvegetarian food and meat other than beef, and at the bottom those who eat beef. In fact, due to the need to survive in extreme poverty, lower castes, and in particular the *dalit*, have developed, over time, dishes that not only include meat but also blood and offal. Among low-caste consumers of meat, the poorest of the poor, those who could not afford any form of freshly slaughtered meat and consumed carrion, were the object of particularly intense opprobrium.

However, besides lower caste Hindus, Christians and Muslims also consume meat and, more specifically, beef. Consumption of meat is not uncommon in the southern states of India, which resent any attempt by the central government at limiting it as a threat to their cultural specificities. Beef is also widely consumed in the northeastern states of Meghalaya and Nagaland.

The latter state has also recently been shaken by a controversy between those who favor and those who oppose the consumption of dog meat. In the summer of 2020, the Nagaland government banned the import and trade of such meat, revealing tensions between supporters of traditional customs and defenders of animal rights, which inevitably got entangled in debates about caste, class, and racism focusing on local tribal communities.[21] The tensions surrounding food consumptions are exploited in broader political disputes about who is really Indian, such as those that followed the government's passage of a law helping non-Muslim illegal immigrants from Muslim-majority countries acquire citizenship while ignoring Muslim ones.[22]

Meat-eating customs have surfaced in other countries as litmus tests to define who belongs and who doesn't. A certain amount of soul searching is taking place around the high amount of meat currently consumed in Poland. Upwardly mobile citizens—especially urban ones—are increasingly aware that too much meat is not good for you. Among them, the number of vegetarians and vegans is on the rise, as are restaurants catering to them, with Warsaw among the most vegan-friendly cities in the world. Especially in rural environments and among the working classes, older generations often scoff at these trends as ridiculous, an expression of foreign influences on Polish culture. While the Polish edition of *Newsweek* dedicated a cover in July 2019 to the "Polish meat problem,"[23] the conservative magazine *Do Rzeczy* titled its October 2019 issue "Who wants to ban us from eating meat?"[24] In a 2018 interview with the German magazine Bild, former Foreign Minister Witold

Waszczykowski criticized previous governments, stating that "the world according to the Marxist pattern had to automatically develop in only one direction—a new mixture of cultures and races, a world of cyclists and vegetarians who use only renewable energy sources and fight all manifestations of religion. It has little to do with traditional Polish values."[25] By conflating cyclists, atheists, and vegetarians, the minister was suggesting that avoiding meat is as alien to Polish identity as trying to find alternative sources of energy in the still coal-based national economy. These new phenomena underlie the sense that the country is besieged by secularism and other corrupting cosmopolitan trends coming from elsewhere. In fact, the conservative Christian magazine *Polonia Christiana* titled the cover of its March-April 2018 issue "Bug on the plate: a culinary revolution," with articles that decried the attempt by the EU (of which Poland is a member) and other not better-specified actors to force people to eat insects.[26]

Similar controversies also took place on the other side of the Atlantic. In April 2021, the *Daily Mail*, a UK tabloid, suggested that, following the new U.S. president Joe Biden's plans to address climate change, "Americans may have to cut their red meat consumption by a whopping 90 percent and cut their consumption of other animal based foods in half," limiting their consumption to a hamburger a month.[27] Citing a study coming out from the University of Michigan, which argued that decreasing red meat intake would contribute to reducing greenhouse gas emissions, former Trump White House economic adviser Larry Kudlow built on the British tabloid allegations to accuse Biden and his climate goals as "anti-beef," predicting a

4th of July where Brussels sprouts would replace burgers for the traditional grilling.[28] Conservative media repeated the accusation, which was immediately amplified on right-wing social media to create a wave of outrage at the attack against sacrosanct American customs and values. A few days later, Fox News apologized for showing a graphic embracing the fake news, but the clarification did little to undo the now widespread perception of plans to address climate change as anti-American.[29] Scientific discussions that were often too abstruse had been simplified and brought to the very tangible and accessible experience of summer grilling. More importantly, the media imbroglio strongly connected red meat consumption with core traditional values and any attempt to limit its consumption with liberal attacks against them.

Meat eating also turned into a political flashpoint when Japan embarked on a path of fast modernization in the second half of the nineteenth century, after the end of its century-long almost total isolation from the Western world. Ideological tensions erased anthropological realities. Meat from wild animals such as boar, deer, and bears had been widely hunted and their meat consumed, particularly in mountain areas and among ethnic minorities. However, following the diffusion of Buddhism from the sixth century CE, beef and dairy became the object of cultural ambivalence. The very need for both religious and civil authorities to repeatedly issue prohibitions against eating meat shows that the custom never totally disappeared, despite a widespread social taboo against meat eating. The routine consumption of meat by Christian missionaries and foreign merchants, designated as corrupters of Japanese mores and spirit, further contributed to entrench meat avoidance.

As Japan was forced to open up to the world after the 1854 peace treaty with the U.S., local reformers identified meat consumption as one of the reasons why Westerners were both physically and politically more powerful. Convincing the population to eat meat became an important goal in the efforts to modernize Japan and raise it to the same level as Western nations. In 1872, the emperor celebrated the New Year by publicly consuming meat. Soon after, a law was passed that allowed Buddhist monks to eat meat as well. The segments of the population that were more attached to traditional behaviors did not react well. Antimeat movements spread all over Japan, creating problems for restaurants and butchers. In reality, the tensions went well beyond dietary preferences: at stake was the future of Japan as a nation and the traits the country wanted to embody on the international scene. It took a few decades for meat consumption to turn into a common habit; nowadays most Japanese no longer consider eating it a taboo.

RACIALIZED FOOD

Race and ethnicity also play a key role in determining who belongs to social groupings, ranging from local communities to entire nations. Foods and culinary customs that can be easily identified with racial or ethnic minorities may end up being erased or treated as idiosyncrasies that survive beyond the realm of mainstream acceptability. In Japan, the foodways of the indigenous Ainu communities from the northern island of Hokkaido are considered by most Japanese to be exotic, based as it is on local crops and protein such as deer, salmon, and cod, often stewed or grilled and seasoned with animal or fish fat rather than soy sauce. Criticized by the government at the end of the nineteenth century as a remnant of a past the country was trying to get rid of, Ainu food customs have survived, at times considered little more than ethnographic curiosities, through direct transmission from mothers to daughters.[30] In the last few decades, however, growing interest in local and traditional foodways has brought them back to the attention of national and international gourmets.[31]

The connections between food and race tend to complicate these dynamics when culinary traditions, ingredients, or dishes can be identified with communities that are (or were) barred from full participation in political life or are struggling to gain full equality as citizens. Their foodways may end up stigmatized as unhealthy, uncouth, or at best unworthy of attention. Their contributions to material culture are, at times, denied or made less relevant in order to raise the profile of the mainstream communities that historically appropriated or exploited them. Deeply engrained dynamics of structural racism weigh heavily on determining boundaries between "us" and "them," even when "they" have a legal right to be part of the polity.

Indigenous peoples in Oceania and the Americas, or the Uighurs in Western China, have a much longer history compared to relative newcomers that nevertheless claim cultural superiority and political domination. Their healthy and sustainable traditional foodways, developed over centuries in response to specific local conditions, have been slowly replaced by supposedly "modern" diets, consisting of mass-produced, calorie-heavy but nutrient-poor industrial products.[32] Traditional crops have been abandoned because of low yields or because they are considered of lesser quality or just backward. Their means of survival can be taken away if they collide with the economic interests of more powerful actors: Amazonian tribes have been deprived of the forest in which they hunt or practice traditional forms of agriculture to make space for commodity crops or pastures for cattle.[33] As a consequence, many indigenous communities around the world now suffer from both malnutrition and the high incidence of noncommunicable conditions such as diabetes or obesity.

To remedy such situations, a growing number of native chefs, food experts, and activists have been trying to bring back crops and customs by making them both more relevant to the communities themselves and more visible to and appreciated by outsiders as healthy and sustainable. Chef Sean Sherman, an Oglala Lakota born in South Dakota, has been organizing public events, cooking, and publishing to give visibility to native farming and culinary techniques, wild plant foraging, and other customary means of food production. In so doing, he often has to build on fragments of material culture and oral traditions that survived integration into the contemporary globalized food system.[34]

Things are not easier for communities descending from former enslaved people of African descent, forcibly brought over to the New World between the sixteenth and the early nineteenth centuries to grow commercial crops such as sugarcane or rice.[35] Their level of integration, their social prestige, and their economic status may vary, but they have all struggled—and in many cases are still struggling—to acquire civil rights and equality as citizens. While in the U.S., Brazil, or the Caribbean their presence is hard to ignore, their contribution to the local food culture is not given proper recognition. Bahian cuisine in Brazil is one of the richest on the continent, with traditions that are the culmination of centuries of not always peaceful interactions between the descendants of Africans, indigenous populations, and waves of immigrants from all over their world. *Acarajé* (black-eye peas and shrimp fritters), *moquecas* (seafood stews cooked in coconut milk and palm oil), or the okra-based *caruru* condiment are considered delicious, but at the same time criticized as too heavy and unhealthy for frequent consumption.[36] In countries like Costa Rica, Mexico, or Peru, the very existence of communities of African descent is not fully acknowledged, and their past is not considered as constitutive to the national identity. Although their food may be appreciated, it is often perceived as something different, easily becoming an object of curiosity or a tourist attraction for both locals and foreigners.

In the U.S., African Americans have contributed enormously to the formation of regional cuisines. Enslaved communities grew, cooked, and served food to their masters, all while elaborating their own culinary traditions and carving out spaces of autonomy and agency in a system designed to exploit and crush them. The history of Black chefs in the White House or the centrality of African Americans in the development of the hospitality and catering industries in the U.S. have only recently been the objects of research and public debate.[37] The status of African American cuisine has, in fact, been subject to continuous negotiation.[38] When, during the first decades of the twentieth century, southern African Americans with a rural background moved en masse to the North to escape the horrors of Jim Crow, their foodways appeared strange and coarse, not only to white northerners but to Blacks as well. Only in the 1960s and 1970s were those dishes and traditions reevaluated as comforting and culturally relevant expressions of "soul food," though political and religious movements such as the Black Panthers and the Nation of Islam dubbed them "slave food," unhealthy and removed from the African roots of the community.[39] Among white Americans, there is a certain tendency to group all African American cuisines into an undistinguished mass regardless of location, class, and religion, with specialties such as fried chicken or gumbo as their symbols. Decades of disdain toward their beloved eating customs has made many African Americans uncomfortable about eating fried chicken or watermelon in the presence of white people, not wanting to confirm racist stereotypes.

When exclusionary gastronativism grows out of classism, racism, ethnic, or religious intolerance, the enemy to be discounted, disenfranchised, and exploited is domestic, although it often connects with similar attitudes elsewhere. Debates are bound to unfold about who belongs to any given community in the first place, generating effective, and at times, violent forms of exclusions. In a zero-sum-game worldview, those who demand equality are a threat to the acquired privileges of the social groupings that identify themselves as legitimate representative of a whole city, region, or even nation. These may end up questioning the very humanity of their less powerful but still fear-provoking foes. And what better way to debase them than pointing to coarseness, low quality, unhealthiness, or even impurity in what they eat? For better or worse, what we ingest determines who we are.

Although the political scene of individual countries may be the main background for these dynamics to unfold, the underlying conflicts are activated by economic and social issues that operate worldwide and have their roots in the current form of globalization, with its growing inequalities and the fear connected with them. That does not mean that the anthropological and cultural fodder for the anxieties expressed by exclusionary gastronativism is novel. On the contrary, long-seated tensions are particularly convenient for generating debates, strategies, and ideological campaigns. Once again, controversies about food are rarely just about food.

Gastronativism provides us with a suitable lens to better understand how current local and national debates spill over and connect with similar tensions and disputes around the world. Indigenous chefs trying to safeguard, support, or highlight the culinary traditions of their communities often collaborate with other chefs that face similar challenges elsewhere. African American chefs strive to find a common language and share similar goals with Afro-Brazilian chefs or even with those in the African countries from which their ancestors came.[40] These conversations have the potential to stimulate communities of African descent to get interested in food cultures in other locations, as the emergence at different times of pan-African points of views and practices suggests. Dialogue can generate intercommunal and transnational solidarities that resist exclusionary gastronativism and the political ideologies that exploit it.

Not all forms of gastronativism work according to the exclusionary patterns we have examined in this this chapter. Identification with a community and attachment to an "us," often generating a strong desire to support and defend it, does not necessarily imply the exclusion, exploitation, or debasement of others. As we will see in the next chapter, the targets of nonexclusionary forms of gastronativism tend to be more powerful and have access to greater financial means than those involved in different forms of resistance. The large transnational corporations, international organizations, or global financial powerhouses that nonexclusionary gastronativist organizations and movements oppose have the means to fight back quite effectively. And they often do.

Chapter Two

TOWARD A BETTER FUTURE

NONEXCLUSIONARY GASTRONATIVISM

IN 2015, Milan, Italy, was abuzz with the World Expo, an international exhibition that has been taking place every year in different locations since 1851. The theme of the 2015 edition was "Feeding the Planet, Energy for Life." National governments, public and private institutions, organizations, and businesses from all over the world built pavilions that showcased what was happening in terms of food, sustainability, and innovation at the global level. The controversy started on May 19, on the occasion of the grand opening of the Slow Food pavilion.[1] Slow Food was planning to have a visible presence as one of the most important international food associations in the world, with hundreds of local and national chapters. After all, its manifest goal since its launch in the late 1980s in Italy is to promote "good, clean, and fair" food for everybody.[2] Carlo Petrini, its founder and president, critiqued the organizers of the World Expo for allowing McDonald's to participate. He was reported stating:

"In front of those who sell meat in a sandwich for euro 1.20, how do you explain the value and the prices of those who raise and produce according to certain criteria?"

McDonald's retort came quick through a press release: "We wonder why those who proclaim the importance of biodiversity do not agree on the idea of diversity of supply, and especially do not demonstrate respect for people's freedom and ability to choose. . . . We are pleased and proud to serve 6,000 affordable meals of good quality at the Expo, with ingredients that come from Italian farmers. . . . Thousands of people chose us freely, maybe after passing to visit the immense, sad and little known Slow Food pavilion."[3] The terms of the controversy were clear: McDonald's defended the affordability of its offer and consumers' individual choices in a free market—an argument the company has made when accused of contributing to health problems among its customers. Moreover, in this specific case, it presented itself as down-to-earth and fun against the supposedly stuffy and elitist approach embraced by Slow Food, which supports and highlights culinary practices and ingredients that can be quite a bit more expensive. These arguments resonated powerfully in Italy, where many citizens were reeling under the hardships imposed on them by a long, and apparently unbeatable, economic crisis.

McDonald's and Slow Food had already publicly vented their differences. The opening of a McDonald's store in a historical neighbor of Rome back in 1986 was one of the motivations for the success of the newly founded association. The two organizations clashed again around local provisioning in 2010, when the then Italian minister of agriculture, Luca Zaia, signed an agreement with the fast food company to introduce sandwiches featuring Italian ingredients such as artichokes and Asiago cheese. Slow Food pointed out that McDonald's did not pay food producers fairly, a matter as important as the origin of the ingredients. McDonald's buys many of its ingredients from within the countries where it operates, partly to satisfy local preferences and to soften its image as a transnational and soulless corporation, partly to reduce transportation and logistics costs, and partly to defuse possible problems regarding religious and other dietary matters (no pork in Muslim countries, no beef in India, etc.). The World Expo controversy with Slow Food extended to labor issues, as McDonald's hiring and personnel policy, together with the low wages it pays to its employees, have been a hot issue for decades. The company pointed out that, in Italy, its employees are hired under the national collective contract for the tourism sector, many with indefinite contracts.

The back-and-forth between an American-based company that has turned into a transnational corporation and an Italian association that is also very visible internationally happened during a global exhibition. The debate took place against the background of issues related to the neoliberal model of globalization: Slow Food was presenting McDonald's as an intruder that prioritizes profit and has a negative impact on local food systems around the world in terms of agrobiodiversity, cultural identity, erasure of local specificities, environmental damage, labor exploitation, and health issues. The implications were much broader than the corporation's presence at the 2015 World Expo and its operations in a specific country, Italy (which happens to be one of the birthplaces of the Mediterranean diet—supposedly, the antithesis of fast food).

In this antagonism, is it easy to recognize a David vs. Goliath narrative in which everyday people get together to resist a much stronger, better organized, and richer enemy. In reality, Slow Food is far from powerless: over the years, it has succeeded in building a network that spans the entire globe and provides political clout and great access to media. Slow Food also publishes and translates its own material into several languages, counting on its members to spread it far and wide.

These dynamics are different from the forms of gastronativism we have explored so far. While the "us" vs. "them" tension is clearly visible, Slow Food's strategies and undertakings neither purposely intend to exclude anybody nor embrace a zero-sum game worldview. They are not about defending privileges, neither do they aim to limit access to equal rights. On the contrary, they explicitly strive for greater fairness and inclusivity. Slow Food is a political project, as it works toward a future in which individuals and communities can make choices regarding food and its impact on jobs, health, and the environment.

Similar attitudes can be observed in movements and organizations that, in different ways, fight against globalization to achieve equality, emotional well-being, and physical health for as many people as possible: antiglobalization organizations, loosely organized "food movements," alternative food networks, associations (like Slow Food), as well as food justice and food sovereignty movements focused on access to food as a right and fighting for farmers' and food producers' rights to self-determination. While acknowledging the existence of boundaries and tribalism, the goal of these very diverse groupings is to weaken or erase them. They want to expand the "us" involved in political participation and determining the future: the ultimate goal is for everybody to have a say about what grows in the fields, what can be found in stores, and what reaches consumers' tables. They all emphasize personal and communal experiences to establish closer relations between food producers and consumers. They tend to oppose the massification and loss of cultural and culinary diversity brought about by the protagonists of neoliberal globalization, from biotech firms to the food industry.

Thanks to technological advancements, these far-reaching and powerful globalizing forces operate at a transnational level, even if gastronativist activism may encounter them at the local, regional, or national level. It takes a second for a hedge fund investor in Melbourne to buy commodities in Mumbai. It is easy for a biotech company to set up shop in far-flung corners of the world, sending bioprospectors into forests to look for the next superfood. Industrial food conglomerates succeed in selling their products, from chips to candy, at the tiniest corner stores in the most remote locations. Much of their strength derives precisely from their worldwide outreach. These are foes that time and time again have shown they do not care about local communities and they are ready to squash them to pursue their political goals, material gains, or financial profit. As a consequence, movements opposing them are forced to think and plan at a global level, often beyond the horizon of nations-states, even when their interventions are local.

Such movements have historical precedents: in the late eighteenth and early nineteenth century in England, individuals and organizations that opposed slavery launched a boycott of sugar, at the time mostly produced by enslaved people, as a way to shake the economic foundations of the commodity since efforts focusing on its ethical aspects were not successful.[4] At the time, England was a truly global imperial power, with products, people, and money flowing in the country. Although the antislavery boycott focused on national politics, it had an impact all over the empire; the consequences of the abolition of slavery were felt worldwide, all the way to the newly independent U.S.[5] Although media were limited compared to today's technology, the movement used the press to spread its ideas, also using cartoons and visual methods to try and talk to the masses. As we will see, such strategies are still very much in place.

FIGHT THE POWER!

Open waters can be treacherous, especially when you throw in your lot with sea creatures. In February 2013, an inflatable boat deployed a wire-reinforced rope with the goal of disabling the rudder and the propeller of the *Yushin Maru*, a Japanese whaling vessel. The inflatable boat had come from the *Bob Barker*, part of the Sea Shepherd Australia fleet, which then collided with both the *Yushin Maru* and its supply tanker.[6] Sea Shepherd is an activist organization whose goal is to stop whaling worldwide, often clashing with Japanese fishing ships. The Australian authorities accused the Japanese fishermen of entering

Australian territorial water, of ramming Sea Shepherd vessels in the Southern Ocean near Antarctica, and of using water cannons and concussion grenades against the activists. The Japanese government countered that it was actually the Australians who attacked first.

That was just one incident in the ongoing battle between sea conservation activists and whalers hunting the mammals despite a global moratorium on commercial whaling adopted in 1982 by the International Whaling Commission. The moratorium has been extended to all whale species starting from the 1985/1986 season.[7] The Save the Whales movement started in the 1960s as part of the broader, nascent environmental movement. In 1961, the newly founded World Wildlife Fund identified the protection of whales as one of its objectives, culminating in 1994 with the establishment of a 50 million square km Southern Ocean Whale Sanctuary.[8] "Save the Whales" bumper stickers, T-shirts, and merchandise could be found everywhere, as conservationist groups multiplied, some of them embracing radical ideas that did not discount direct action. The American Cetacean Society and other conservation organizations such the Humane Society International, the Sierra Club, and Greenpeace also participated in the effort to protect the cetaceans. The Sea Shepherd Conservation Society, involved in the *Yushin Maru* incident, is in fact a splinter group of Greenpeace that chose to launch interventions at sea.

Despite the moratorium, Japanese whalers exploit a loophole in the agreement that allows the mammals to be killed for scientific research. As whale meat is consumed in Japan and cartilage, blubber, and oil are used in pharmaceuticals and health supplements, fishermen use this ruse to meet the market demand. Norway continues commercial whaling as well, while Iceland stopped its activities in 2019.⁹ The issue is further complicated by the fact that the moratorium allows for subsistence whaling by indigenous peoples as an expression of their culture and a response to their nutritional needs, as long as their fishing activities do not endanger the cetacean population in the long term. The Chukotka populations of Far Eastern Russia, Canadian Inuit, Alaskan natives, and the Makah of Washington State in the U.S., as well as whaling communities in Indonesia and the Caribbean, have claimed this exception. Indigenous populations are both threatened by commercial whalers and antagonized by activists. Similar tensions have developed around commercial tuna fishing in the Mediterranean, as well as around traditional tuna fishing methods such as the *mattanza* in Sicily and the *almadraba* in Spain, considered excessively cruel.

Environmental movements have become global: activists belong to different nationalities, ethnicities, and classes. Their organizations are often transnational, and so is the fishing industry they oppose. Even when fighting individual ships or companies, they are taking on the whole category, and their demands are far-reaching, aiming at structural and long-term changes. However, their worldview differs from the zero-sum game we observed in exclusionary gastronativism: they assume the position of those who fight for justice, in this case for the whales and, through them, for the whole environment, which is conflated with the future of humanity. They feel that whales are victims of powerful and well organized forces that operate for their own profit and to the detriment of all others, including fellow human beings.

These forces are, in turn, the expression of actors in the food system that prioritize the exploitation of nonrenewable resources, deny the impact of negative externalities or refuse to assume responsibility for them, and favor the unbridled push-and-pull of supply and demand in the free markets, all core traits of neoliberal globalization. On their end, environmentalists draw from the ideologies, strategies, and practices of the antiglobalization movements, which made their first noticeable appearance in Seattle in 1999 with massive demonstrations against that year's World Trade Organization (WTO) meeting. Activists fight to avoid the tragedy of the commons. Destructive greed needs to be curtailed by the community of the downtrodden, a diverse assemblage that includes responsible humans who care for and look after the environment and their own kind (including their foes, even if they don't care), animals, and all nonliving actors that ensure the ecological balance of nature and its long-term sustainability. These activists see themselves as part of food chains for which they take responsibility, giving up unsustainable forms of consumption for the common good.

Depending on the battles, environmentalists may co-opt indigenous populations as allies or critique them as adversaries, although the rhetoric and the strategies they use in those cases are very different from the verbal and physical attacks they wage against transnational industries. Antiglobalists, environmentalists, and human right activists have joined forces, for instance, to support the indigenous populations of the Amazon in their battle against the timber, mining, cattle, and agrobusiness companies that continue clearing large areas of rainforest to expand their production. While under the presidencies of Luiz Inácio Lula da Silva and Dilma Rousseff their activities had slowed down, under Jair Bolsonaro deforestation hit a twelve-year high in 2020.[10] The Brazilian president is known for his outright racist proclamations, which tend to exclude the indigenous populations from actual citizenship and even question their very presence in large swaths of the country. Bolsonaro overtly indicated indigenous reserves and *quilombolas* (territories belonging to descendants of African enslaved communities) as an obstacle to agribusiness.[11] As in the case of fisheries, it is not difficult for activists to point out connections between local companies, local and foreign land owners, and transnational businesses that need raw materials.

Similar tensions have developed around oil palm cultivation, which has expanded in Africa and Southeast Asia. Forests are being destroyed to make room for plantations that reduce local biodiversity and have a negative impact on soil, water, and climate, all while endangering species such as the orangutans. Large areas are cleared with the support of local and national authorities, starved for revenue and raw materials for export. The decisions are often made without the permission of local communities, which end up as exploited workers in the plantations.[12] The issue is connected with land grabbing, a phenomenon that has expanded as arable land is increasingly considered to be a solid investment for sovereign funds, pension and hedge funds, endowments, and even wealthy individuals.[13] The financialization of food commodities and food production has turned agricultural land into a valuable asset, regardless of the social and economic consequences at the local level.

Probably the food-related issue that has provoked the most intense political reactions is the cultivation of genetically modified organisms (GMOs) and their inclusion in both animal feed and products for human consumption. Genetic modification has been mainly applied to commercial crops such as wheat, soybeans, and corn, grown in huge quantities and traded internationally, with the goal of increasing yields regardless of the widespread use of herbicides and fertilizers (which are often patented by the same companies that own the GMO patents). It is undoubtedly a global issue in which powerful transnational actors (private companies, international institutions, research organizations, and financial interests) have played a central role.

No matter what the research about the safety of GM crops for human consumption indicates, growing numbers of consumers and activists do not trust them, also pointing to the environmental risks in terms of loss of agrobiodiversity and the legal issues related to intellectual property infringement that many farmers around the world routinely face when GM biological material ends up in their fields. The expansion of GM crops has caused the abandonment of plant varieties that were labor intensive or provided low yields, even when they were well adapted to specific environmental conditions or local dynamics of production. Thanks to NAFTA (now the United States–Mexico–Canada Agreement), in Mexico, drought-resisting varieties of corn have been replaced by foreign high-yield ones that are more expensive and less adaptive.[14] However, heirloom varieties are being "rediscovered" because of their resilience to climate change, their quality, and their flavor. Large efforts are in place to safeguard and reintroduce value-added products, often marketing them internationally at higher prices.[15]

Farmers around the world have shown diverse attitudes toward GMOs. In the U.S., large industrial farms have largely embraced them. In the European Union, although strict protocols have been imposed, most consumers still refuse them, making their cultivation unappealing and forcing food producers to clearly signal the presence of GM ingredients on packaging. Depending on the context, farmers and local authorities may also support activists' efforts to curb the cultivations of GM crops. In 2010 a group of No Global activists burned GM corn fields in the Italian region of Veneto, applauded by the local governor (and condemned by the national minister of agriculture).[16] In 2013, the Hungarian minister for rural development approved the torching of around five hundred acres of GM corn planted with Monsanto seeds.[17]

Farmers would not seem to be automatically against the use of GM seeds if it makes economic sense. In India, a market for "stealth" seeds for cotton and eggplants has expanded.[18] Farmers crossbreed GM and non-GM seeds without paying any royalties to the patent owners and establish parallel networks for distribution and sale. In 2004, the minister of agriculture Sharad Pawar brought the issue to Parliament, as the farmers' behavior jeopardizes any unified government policy on the issue.[19] Despite the complexity of the issue in its local manifestations, anti-GMO activists and organizations have developed common strategies, language, and initiatives that are increasingly shared across borders and adapted to different contexts.

IMAGINING A DIFFERENT FOOD SYSTEM

The strategies we have examined so far have strong and clear political content: their explicit goal is to oppose and change aspects of the socioeconomic status quo, either gradually or through radical measures. However, not all nonexclusionary gastronativist movements are overtly political. Some focus rather on establishing alternative food networks that promote more equitable and sustainable forms of food production, distribution, and consumption compared to mainstream commercial enterprises. Such initiatives are embedded in local communities, contributing to civic society building. They include community gardens, farmers' markets, farm-to-table restaurants, back-to-the-land migrations, ecovillages, food coops, and community-supported agriculture, in which consumers agree in advance with farmers to buy their harvest or a portion of it, usually delivered at agreed-upon intervals. Although these endeavors are implicitly political, as they favor social and economic arrangements that differ from the current ones, they are decidedly low-key and avoid direct political confrontation. Without asking for radical reforms of social and economic systems, they variously oppose the disappearance of family farms, the exploitation of labor, the misuse of resources such as land

and water, and the overall globalization of the food system, which they identify with the power of heavily financialized transnational food corporations.

The preference for buying local has been gaining ground among urbanites that feel cut off from the countryside surrounding their cities: it is at times easier (and cheaper) to buy goods whose origin is unclear than to purchase foods from close-by farmers and artisans. Growing numbers of eaters and shoppers, at times referring to themselves as "locavores," try to limit their consumption of products coming from faraway places, not only to reduce the carbon footprint connected to long-haul transportation but also to reaffirm their desire to connect with their own places and communities. This decision may imply turning to local plant varieties and animal breeds, rediscovering traditional techniques of cultivation that are adapted to local conditions, and changing one's culinary habits. However, the risk of the "local trap" is always lurking.[20] Small-scale food productions are not automatically more environmentally sustainable, more democratic, or more equitable than far-reaching networks. The priorities of all stakeholders involved and the power relations among them is more crucial in determining the characteristics of local food arrangements than their scale and their connection with more distant places.

Alternative food networks and locavorism are the most ideological expression of what has been characterized as a "food movement" or "good food movement" that encompasses producers, distributors, consumers, various intermediaries such as restaurateurs, food critics, and the media, as well as international associations like Slow Food and think tanks such as

Food First and Food Tank. Still budding and mostly uncoordinated, the food movement is increasingly visible in many countries.[21] Focusing on diverse issues and, at times, representing contradictory interests, it expresses a set of ideas and practices on a spectrum that stretches from politically engaged and collective activism to individual behaviors based on the principle that private purchase choices can have an impact on the system. It is the "vote with your wallet" attitude, which risks overlooking the efficacity (and necessity) of organized action tackling structural issues that require direct participation in the political life of the community. Paradoxically, those who pine for tastier, more nutritious, more sustainable food may be unwittingly buying into approaches that prioritize individual preferences and the effectiveness of the free market to distribute and optimize resources while discounting the need for public and governmental interventions to foster better coordination among stakeholders, support the disadvantaged, and introduce regulations.

The values and norms underlying choices and strategies in the food movement are far from being uniform across the board, as participants vary in terms of class, education, geographical location, race and ethnicity, financial situation, as well as age and generation. The "us" consists of all those for whom food is important in determining their identity and well-being as individuals and citizens, along with farmers, artisans, fishermen, and other food workers. If the goal is changing what and how we eat, it is necessary to involve as many individuals and communities as possible, respecting their differences and their peculiarities. The participants in the food movement tend to see themselves as having the common good at heart, even when their actions are private and based on personal preferences.

It is not always smooth sailing. At times, power differences in terms of class, gender, ethnicity, or race are glossed over.[22] Members of the cosmopolitan elites, usually urban, highly educated, and with noticeable spending power, focus on the defense of locality, traditions, and artisans to react against the loss of quality, the massification, and the erasure of food cultures brought on by globalization. However, they can be blind to their own biases, which might exclude or ignore large parts of the population.[23] As a consequence, their positions about what is tasteful, appropriate, healthy, authentic, and, above all, affordable may be resented as elitist and contrary to the community ethos and interests, eliciting both the critique of food justice activists and reactions from exclusionary gastronativists, as in the case of the opposition to Polish vegetarians we examined in the previous chapter.

FOOD SOVEREIGNTY

Strategies and interventions aimed at achieving systemic and structural changes vary depending on who is involved. Often concentrating on local dynamics, especially in urban environments, food justice activists focus on food as a human right and demand fair access to healthy and affordable food for all, included groups marginalized on the base of gender, economic status, citizenship, or race. Family farmers and small holders in low- and middle-income countries, including those belonging to indigenous populations, have also felt the need to take their future in their own hands. They have established organizations that are focused on their specific necessities and priorities, even if some of their goals often overlap with antiglobalization activism, environmentalism, and the food movement. The political perspective that such farmer movements embrace is known as food sovereignty, which indicates the right of communities at all scales, from a village to a whole nation, to democratic self-determination of the food system they want to live in.

The U.S. Food Sovereignty Alliance explains these movements as "growing from the bottom up, from the farmers, fishers, indigenous peoples and landless workers most impacted by global hunger and poverty. Food sovereignty goes well beyond ensuring that people have enough food to meet their physical needs. It asserts that people must reclaim their power in the food system by rebuilding the relationships between people and the land, and between food providers and those who eat."[24]

The best organized expression of this approach is La Via Campesina ("the Farmers' Path" in Spanish), officially launched in 1993 in Mons, Belgium. From the start, its explicit goal was to develop a common vision and effective strategies to counteract the increasingly globalized agribusiness and agricultural policies that national governments and local authorities were imposing, often inspired by neoliberal principles and practices promoted by the World Bank and International Monetary Fund. La Via Campesina made itself globally visible during the 1999 protests against the WTO, pushing for agrarian reforms and highlighting the damage inflicted on rural communities by free trade. A self-governing, autonomous, and variegated movement, La Via Campesina coordinates grassroots peasant organizations around the world and aims at reconstructing and reviving a shared peasant identity. Its combative attitudes express themselves though demonstrations, no-holds-barred political debates, and direct actions. Some of its member organizations support territorial autonomy without negotiations with national governments, at times, refusing to recognize their authority or even their legitimacy.

Over the years, the meaning of food sovereignty has become more precise, culminating in the definition included in the Declaration of Nyéléni, approved in 2007 by delegates from eighty countries at the Forum for Food Sovereignty in Sélingué, Mali. In the declaration, food sovereignty is explained as "the right of peoples to healthy and culturally appropriate food produced through ecologically sound and sustainable methods, and their right to define their own food and agriculture systems. It puts the aspirations and needs of those who produce, distribute and consume food at the heart of food systems and policies rather than the demands of markets and corporations. It defends the interests and inclusion of the next generation."[25]

The concepts of food sovereignty and food justice are relevant in the farm labor movements that, around the world, defend paid workers from exploitation, often dealing with migration issues, racism, and social isolation. Food sovereignty is also a powerful framework for the indigenous organizations that are trying to bring back traditional knowledge, practices, and crops as a form of resistance against the vestiges of colonization and the penetration of global actors that threaten the cultural and physical survival of entire indigenous communities. Last but not least, seeds have been identified as a central battleground for food sovereignty, as intellectual property has expanded to cover increasingly broader matters, from genetic engineering to the appropriation of genetic resources. Activists such as Vandana Shiva have been organizing farmers (especially women) to focus on local varieties, gathering and selecting their seeds while making them available to the community. Organizations like Open Source Seed Initiative (OSSI) are establishing seed sharing mechanisms that would apply the principles of the Creative Commons and open source software to plant breeding.[26]

Growing numbers of communities and individuals are getting involved in issues as diverse as whales and seeds in order to achieve fairer food systems. In exclusionary gastronativism, instead, the effort is to underline the differences among communities with the goal of maintaining privileges and a status quo that are experienced as threatened. In both cases, food proves extremely effective in activating civic passions at various scales, even when the real enemy—neoliberal globalization—is not necessarily identified or recognized. Why does food have such a power over us, often constituting a central flashpoint in cultural and social debates? How can it be so easily used as an ideological tool to draw us to all kinds of political projects? That is what we will be exploring in part 2.

PART TWO

THE POWER OF FOOD

Chapter Three

FOOD AND IDENTITY

EVERY TIME I stroll in the Trionfale market, in my Rome neighborhood, I cannot help but enjoy the variety of familiar foods, their aromas, the calls of the vendors, the colors of fruits and vegetables. It never fails: after so many years living elsewhere, it still feels like home. The same goes for the dishes that my mother prepares year after year for the holidays and special occasions: they taste like home—my Roman home. Although I have learned how to make them (of course, not as well as my mom), I never prepare them when I am in the U.S. They belong to another place, to other events. They tell stories that are personal and emotional for me and for those I cook for or eat with. Over time, I have developed my own menu, a new language to speak to my American life and my American family. Close friends know I don't follow recipes and enjoy experimenting, but less intimate acquaintances somehow expect some performance of culinary Italianness when I invite them over. I have gotten the question: "Is this really Italian?," as though being Italian is all there is to me. I am also a chocolate fiend; I have lived and traveled abroad, so my comfort food includes Spanish, French, Chinese, Mexican, and American dishes; I hate throwing out food, so I become particularly creative when it comes to making good use of leftovers. And I could go on . . .

My point is that food helps to define who we are, both to ourselves and to those with whom we produce, prepare, cook, eat, and dispose of food. Food is performative: by cooking things we are familiar with and that are able to comfort us, we reassure ourselves of our own identities while projecting the image we think the world should or expects to see. Even when we have to cook because we are responsible for feeding others or because it is our job, or when we are forced to eat to be polite or to please others, it is hard to avoid feelings about it. Food is fundamental not only because it ensures our survival but also because ingestion and incorporation—as well as what we refuse to incorporate, for instance, when we boycott, fast, or struggle with an eating disorder—constitute a key component of our connection with reality outside our body. Food mediates the most intimate aspects of our lives with the world out there. It influences us as a visible and tangible marker of power, cultural capital, social class, gender, ethnicity, and religion.

When we cook and eat (or reject eating), we establish categories and create boundaries that can exclude those we consider "others." That is why food is able to express belonging and community at various scales, from the very local to the national and the transnational.[1] At the same time, it also reminds us that separation from aspects of reality we would prefer to keep at a distance is just wishful thinking. In fact, food connects our most personal experiences and our bodies to global systems. To some Romans, a certain lack of interest—at times, the refusal—to buy okra in their neighborhood markets from immigrant vendors may express a preference for familiar foods that reflect an established, local identity. On the other hand, my personal interest for the exotic vegetable could articulate a desire to engage with the world at large, nostalgia for a trip abroad and the memories that come with it, or maybe just the fact that I have lived in places where okra is part of everyday cooking. The immigrant vendor I buy okra from in Rome has a stall at the neighborhood market, and the vegetable, not native to Italy and rarely grown there, is available: these are clear indications of food globalization. In reality, crops and food products have been transferred around the world since the inception of agriculture: wheat, domesticated in the Mediterranean area, found its way to China and was grown by the time the first written texts emerged around the end of the second millennium BCE; conversely, rice traveled from China to Southeast Asia and westward to India, Persia, and the Mediterranean world. The isolation between the Old and the New World came to an end in the late fifteenth century with the Columbian exchange: corn, tomatoes, beans, and peppers were adopted from Spain to China, while olives, grapes, wheat, and onions were brought to the Americas.

What has changed in recent decades is the speed of the phenomenon, due to improved and intensified trade and the visibility communication technologies allow. Consumers and marketers are constantly looking for new superfoods that quickly become widely available and accessible; while their qualities are touted in the media, visual social media explain what they look like and how they should be prepared and enjoyed. Well-off, privileged consumers like myself have the opportunity to taste specialties from all over the world (like okra in my Roman neighborhood market), enjoying novel practices and innovative taste categories. Food lovers may express their distinction, refinement, and cosmopolitanism by displaying familiarity with foreign specialties. These behaviors are not limited to the Global North: despite the high prices due to substantial import taxes, wine is gaining popularity among gourmets in India, while cheese has found its place in upscale delicatessens in China. Such preferences and habits, although personal, inevitably convey meanings that can be read and channeled politically: what do consumers express about their ideas about food and the food system by choosing to shop at a big box store, at a supermarket, at a corner store, at a gourmet store, or at a farmers' market? What vision of society is embedded in the preference for exotic, expensive products coming from far away, as opposed to a predilection for local ones or to the capacity to move effortlessly between the formers and the latter?

Culinary tourism, which folklorist Lucy Long has presented as the exploration of other cultures through their food, is now a popular practice.[2] Mexican, Chinese, Japanese, and Italian stores and restaurants allow eaters to have some exposure to those culinary traditions. However, while many approach unfamiliar foods with an honest desire to better understand the cultures behind them, others may enjoy a specialty from a foreign community while maintaining racist attitudes toward its members. Numerous U.S. citizens who gladly consume tacos and enchiladas also support the building of a wall between Mexico and their country. Philosopher Lisa Heldke has pointed out that through such "exotic appetites" eaters from communities in more powerful positions are able to impose their interpretations and preferences to the migrants cooking for them.[3] Black feminist scholar bell hooks has criticized "eating the other" as a way to spice up what could be experienced as the blandness of whiteness.[4]

When we are traveling or going to an ethnic restaurant for the first time, we can be adventurous, ordering the very dishes we are less familiar with or challenging ourselves and each other to ingest whatever seems more exotic and dangerous, like in the Japanese tradition of eating *fugu* fish. Depending on our mood, our experiences, and the context, we may instead try to avoid any mysterious fare. After all, we do tend to consider what does not fit within our categories of the edible as potentially polluting or disgusting. Moreover, we are constantly aware that even familiar foods can be both sources of nourishment and very dangerous substances if taken in excessive quantities, badly cooked, or just clumsily chosen. Danger and death are inscribed in food and the pleasure that may come from it.

We can push our culinary boundaries because, as social scientist Claude Fischler pointed out, our physiology as omnivorous animals allows us to consume a wide variety of substances. We are always attracted to the discovery of opportunities to feed ourselves, but we are also fearful that a new addition to our diet could make us sick or kill us. It is what Fischler called the "omnivorous dilemma" between "neophilia," the desire for the new, and "neophobia," the fear that the new is potentially dangerous.[5] When we are exposed to exotic or foreign dishes, we find ourselves in the realm of the uncertain, facing challenges that shake the culinary points of reference that allow us to know what is what, what is good for us, and what is not. Culture and nature reveal blurred boundaries, with the nourishing and the venomous separated by leaky edges.

These complexities and contradictions, often accompanied by anxieties and fears, can easily take political undertones, even for those among us who would prefer to remain apolitical. They also explain how the cultural flexibility of eating and its infinite meanings are easily recruited in support of strategies and activities with very different purposes and meanings, as it happens in gastronativism. Food is a highly symbolic realm subject to discourse and interpretation, and, as Lévi-Strauss has pointed out, it is as exclusive a human behavior as language: "Cooking, it has never been sufficiently emphasized, is with language a truly universal form of human activity: if there is no society without a language, nor is there any which does not cook in some manner at least some of its food."[6] Just like language, food communicates and generates meaning. More important, it prompts us to interpret and judge the meaning it carries. We can use it to express ourselves but also to read into how others cook and eat. Because it contributes to defining our identity and is the object of profound ambivalences, food can easily turn into a tangible mark for both communal identity and otherness, a symbol that can be physically ingested or refused.

FOOD TRADITIONS AND CULINARY HERITAGE

One of the most powerful modes through which food gets co-opted in gastronativist projects, in both exclusionary and non-exclusionary approaches, is through ideas, values, and practices revolving around "tradition" and "heritage." Tradition can be understood as a field of social activity in which a community identifies and selects practices and customs from previous generations that, in some form, are still performed in the present, both in everyday life and special occasions. These elements are attributed particular significance, and their preservation is considered central to the continuation of the community. In these processes, historical facts may be taken out of context and shaped into narratives that establish clear, direct, and unchanging links between a community and its past: "We have always eaten this"; "This is how we cook." As a process of evaluation and selection of ideas and practices from previous times, tradition emerges as a set of beliefs, attitudes, behaviors, and objects that shape the transmission of knowledge and the cultural reproduction of a social grouping.

Traditions both reflect and shape customs. A strong sense of community might not exist prior to the choice of material culture elements that, elevated to constitute tradition, become central to the formation or the consolidation of a shared identity. Politically, these dynamics are formidable. They can be leveraged to build more or less temporary communities at different scales that can be activated in particular situations and with specific goals, calling on individuals and groups to generate fresh and ever-evolving formations. That is the case for the "no GMO" or antiglobalization movements, food sovereignty transnational organizations or local anti-immigrant mobs that can establish bonds among individuals and groups that had no previous relations, while connecting them with similar groups elsewhere.

As social historian Eric Hobsbawm observed, traditions can be "invented" as a "response to novel situations which take the form of reference to old situations, or which establish their own past by quasi-obligatory repetition."[7] As such, they frequently build on the nostalgia for good old days that may have never existed. Moreover, communities and individuals do understand that traditions change over time. The extent to which such alterations are deemed acceptable and not threatening is determined by negotiations both within the community itself and those who are external to it. However, as limited as it may be, awareness about the shifting nature of traditions and communities does not make them less emotionally significant for those who partake in them. For those who feel their daily life threatened by forces that are difficult to understand and on which they have little control, as it happens when facing neoliberal globalization, the past becomes something to prize and safeguard, a source of pride, and an anchor for the reproduction and the defense of cultural identities.

Elements of food traditions—objects and practices—can further be framed as heritage when they are acknowledged as particularly central to the life of a community and its distinctiveness, turning them into a useful tool to reinforce distinction between "insiders" and outsiders, between "us" and "them."[8] Formal processes are frequently established in which institutions are attributed the authority to identify elements of extraordinary cultural value, at times including them in registers, lists, or museums. In the case of food, varieties of plants and animal breeds, recipes, and practices can be transformed into objects for display and exhibition, whether physical or metaphorical.[9] This means that culinary heritage is not something that lies hidden and needs to be uncovered by those who have the expertise and the authority to do so, including governments and—as we will see in chapter 6—actors such as the United Nations Educational, Scientific and Cultural Organization (UNESCO). Heritage is constructed.

Just like tradition, heritage is the outcome of social activities, cultural priorities, and political values. As performance scholar Barbara Kirshenblatt-Gimblett observed, heritage is a mode of cultural production in the present that has recourse to the past, following motivations that have to do with current conditions. It creates value-added industries: objects, dishes, and crafts that are recognized as heritage acquire greater value, particularly when they are displayed or experienced outside their place of origin or turned into tourism resources.[10] While unique crops or animal breeds may be selected and safeguarded as heritage with the goal to ensure agrobiodiversity in the future, they also have the potential to generate economic windfalls in terms of tourism and product sales. Due to its constructed nature, heritage operates within a certain dimension of virtuality, regardless of the presence or the absence of its actual components.[11] This last aspect is particularly relevant because digital and social media—especially visual platforms—have become central to contemporary food culture, which is incessantly mediated: objects, spaces, experiences, and practices are often designed to be instagrammable and aesthetically pleasant.[12] Visual elements not only shape current trends in food culture, but also contribute to defining traditions and heritage even when their original manifestations are no longer there, making them available for political purposes.

REIMAGINING THE PAST

Traditions and heritage acquire greater ideological meaning and emotional weight when current customs are attributed a long history that they may not actually have. In this search for roots, the origin of a dish or a culinary custom attains particular relevance. When a clear origin does not exist, myths emerge, especially around foods that are considered quintessential to the identity of a community, like pasta for Italians or Champagne for Frenchmen. Who invented dried pasta? Was it the Chinese, the Italians, or, as more recent research suggests, Middle Eastern populations? Did Marco Polo bring it to Venice from his travels in the Far East? And who started using durum wheat to make dried pasta? What is the origin of Champagne? Was it a seventeenth-century creation by Dom Perignon, procurer of the abbey of Hautvillers, or is it rather the culmination of a long process that started in the Middle Ages? Has it always tasted the way it does today, or has it evolved over time? In most cases, as food historian Massimo Montanari has observed, origins cannot be pinpointed to a precise moment in the past from which everything stems.[13] Origins are rather like seeds that have the potential to turn into something, but what they actually become depends on myriad factors, historical processes, encounters, and clashes that are serendipitous and fateful, at times uncomfortable and in contrast with received ideas or ideological tenets.

How do Italian anti-immigration advocates deal with the information about the beginnings of their beloved durum dried pasta, which is likely to have first appeared in the Middle East and spread only later to other areas in the Mediterranean? How do American white supremacists react to the evidence that southern rice culture took roots in the New World only thanks to the skills of enslaved people from West Africa, and many of their specialties are tightly connected with African culinary culture? Many in the food movement fetishize the good old days of agriculture, when everything was genuine, food production was local, and agrobiodiversity thrived. In that perspective, technology is treated with suspicion, at times with Luddite undertones. It matters little that farmers of yore who toiled and suffered on the fields were victims of exploitation and often went hungry.

The past is often reconsidered and reimagined to respond to contemporary debates and needs, with little regard for historical facts. When activists of the Lega Nord Party in Italy cooked and distributed polenta on the streets while circulating posters that stated "Yes to polenta, no to couscous," the fact that couscous has been present in Italy since the colonization of Sicily by Muslim populations in the ninth century, well before the arrival of maize from the New World in the sixteenth century, was apparently of no consequence in terms of the emotional and political impact of the message. In 2019, Poland saw a debate about the intention of the government to mark bison and beaver as edible meats, causing the reaction of animal welfare activists and the more liberal sectors of society. Immediately, discussions developed to ascertain if those animals were historically part of Polish culinary traditions—a theme that is closely connected with the role of hunting in contemporary society.

When, in 2020, a paper was published in the journal *Cell* asserting that agriculture developed autonomously in the Indian subcontinent and not through influences coming from the area of today's Iran, Hindu fundamentalists immediately embraced the theory as further proof of the autonomous origins of Indian culture.[14] Thanksgiving traditions in the U.S. have become a central part of the performance of being an American, for those born there and for immigrants alike. The holiday celebrates the sharing of resources between indigenous populations and the British newcomers in the seventeenth century. Although we now know how those encounters actually went, the myth perdures. Moreover, the celebration itself is not that old. When northerners tried to introduce it into southern states after the Civil War, southerners opposed it as a form of cultural imperialism from the winners of the conflict. In fact, Thanksgiving became a national holiday only in 1941, during World War II.

Perceptions people have about food tend to shift over time, influenced by education, class, their exposure to different contexts, and innumerable other factors. The revaluation of food traditions and culinary heritage, treated as expression of diversity and multiculturality, an enrichment for a country's foodscape, has been influenced by trends in global cosmopolitanism that embrace local and traditional foods as a form of educated and class-inflected resistance to mass production and homogenization. These practices have been described as the "gastronomization" of local popular cuisines.[15] An emerging and networked community of cosmopolitan gastronomes, gourmets, and experts, often with high spending power, share similar expectations about what food should taste and look like. Cosmopolitan foodies have developed a specialized language, categories of taste, and, at times, a certain condescension for local and traditional foods when they are produced, prepared, and consumed according to older paradigms that carry connotations of ignorance and backwardness.

In Thailand, recipes from the northeastern region of Isan that were long considered rustic and uninteresting, negatively connected with the masses of immigrants that had moved to large cities from that area, are now cherished by urban gourmets in Bangkok and Chiangmai. Their apparently simple preparations, as well as their distinctive use of unusual ingredients like sticky rice, pork, and rice sausage, reflect the ideals of authenticity and closeness to tradition that gourmets around the world have come to value. If vodka penne and pasta with heavy cream were appreciated in Italy in the 1980s as a sign of cosmopolitan refinement, they are now considered with some disdain or are seasoned with a good dose of irony. Conversely, in the 1960s, for many Italians *pasta e fagioli* (pasta and bean soup) embodied their painful ambivalence between the shame they felt regarding their rural origins, often steeped in poverty, and their desire for a delicious comfort food that nevertheless marked them as backward. Now, *pasta e fagioli* is enjoyed as an authentic symbol of tradition, and chefs do not disdain adding it to their menus—of course, in elevated versions featuring premium ingredients.

Through food traditions and heritage, social actors establish connections between their ideas about the past, their experiences in the present, and their expectations for the future. Traditions open themselves to be integrated in political projects precisely because they are, in many ways, political themselves, in the sense that they participate in determining what a community is and how it sees itself down the line. Individuals and social groupings articulate their identities not only by locating themselves in time but also by judging different periods (as good or bad, crisis or growth). It is important to underline that such perceptions of time go well beyond individual experiences and constitute shared discourses in which some histories (and stories) are privileged over others. A multiplicity of actors contribute to generating judgements about the past, but not all the participants in the process wield the same power or authority in determining what is truly traditional and what is not. Inevitably, some voices are louder and more respected than others.

LOOKING FOR AUTHENTICITY

In contemporary food culture, authenticity has become a central concept alongside tradition and heritage.[16] Authenticity denotes the expected adherence of ingredients, dishes, and customs to an idealized, supposedly original form built on genuineness and the lack of artifice and pretention. It allows consumers to have direct access to the true nature not only of what they eat but also of the people that produce, cook, and serve food to them. Its roots are to be found in time (the past) and in space (specific places). It can also refer to skills and techniques that are embedded in a world of artisans and producers with unique personalities and stories: the opposite of mass production. Despite the sophistication that "authentic" products may display, connotations of "simplicity" and "straightforwardness" remain important, especially when they are identified as exotic and "other."

Because of these characteristics, authenticity constitutes an important component of what Joseph Pine and James Gilmore defined as "experience economy."[17] When consumers buy a product, pay for a service, or participate in an experience, what they are interested in, besides the tangible characteristics of what they get, are the stories, memories, and people behind it. Value is often determined not only by the gustatory traits of a specialty or by the quality of a service but also by their rootedness in identifiable communities, about which information can be acquired. A Thai restaurant feels more authentically Thai if the cook and the staff are recognizably Thai; it is even better when some customers are Thai as well, giving the place the seal of "the real thing."

The ability to distinguish authenticity becomes part of consumers' cultural capital, but the bases for their authority to determine what is authentic remain unclear. One's grandmother's version of a certain recipe inevitably feels more authentic than the one from another family. A Chinese national may feel that Chinese dishes in Spain, Curaçao, or India are not authentic, but those same dishes are likely to feel absolutely authentic to second- or third-generation individuals of Chinese descent. Traditions and authenticity are materialized through regulated and ritualized practices: some deliberately performed, some so engrained to become automatic and "natural." Through them, members of a community define themselves, acknowledged as such by their peers while easily spotting outsiders.

To give order to the never-ending debates about what is traditional and authentic, culinary expertise has emerged that, at times, takes the form of institutions or organizations meant to regulate the characteristics of a certain product. The association of the Neapolitan pizza makers has established rules about authentic Neapolitan pizza, but, as no international pizza police exists yet, pizza keeps on changing and taking new forms. In intellectual property instruments such as geographical indications, with the support of local and national governments, it is the producers themselves who determine the sensory traits, the manufacturing methods, and even the packaging of products whose name has a specific and unique connection with its geographical origin. This is the case for Parmigiano Reggiano from Italy, Champagne from France, argan oil from Morocco, and tequila from Mexico. Only producers from those specific locations who follow agreed-upon regulations can claim authenticity for their goods. As we will see in chapter 7, these matters have economic and legal consequences.

Considering all the negotiations about authenticity in the domestic and public spheres, the most relevant question appears to be not which foods are authentic, but why and how authenticity as a category for judgment and value has become so central in contemporary food culture in general and in gastronativism in particular, which turns it into another ideological tool in political debates.

Although socially constructed, tradition, heritage, and authenticity are not expendable. They are interwoven with individual and communal identities, influencing their emergence and operation and buttressing their stability. They allow social groups to resist neoliberal globalization and its consequences, from mass migrations to free trade. Yet, when accepted blindly, tradition, heritage, and authenticity can become political weapons for discrimination and intolerance. The attachment to one's identity, if it expresses fear of diversity and the defense of boundaries, is likely to generate destructive drives that can be easily channeled into discontent and rage. Even when violence is not in the picture, power and food remain tightly connected.

Chapter Four

FOOD AND POWER

IN LATE October 2020, despite the fact that the COVID-19 pandemic was ravaging the country, the streets of Polish cities were flooded with thousands of people demonstrating against a decision of the national Constitutional Tribunal to restrict reproductive rights, virtually banning any form of legal abortion.[1] Women, but also men, were shouting their anger in public despite threats from radical right-wing nationalists, rebukes from members of the government, and fulminations from the Catholic Church. Their expressions, directed at governing party Prawo i Sprawiedliwość (PiS, Law and Justice), were both playful and confrontational, underlining how the protest was going against the grain and making fun of sanctimoniousness and hypocrisy. The protesters also wrote banners and signs, which they paraded high and visibly so that they could be photographed to multiply their message through traditional newspapers, TV, and social media.

Curiously, many of the taunts aimed at the politicians in power used metaphors and wordplay about food. "Today we will be stewing a duck," read a sign that carried the effigy of Magda Gessler, a famous, larger-than-life female food TV personality. The pun used the assonance between Jarek Kaczyński, the de facto strong man of Polish conservative politics, and *kaczka*, a duck: a powerful man had been transformed into a barnyard fowl, ready to be plucked, cooked, and eaten by a woman. Other signs proclaimed: "Better cottage cheese with raisins than PiS," "PiS is worse than licorice jellybeans," "Jarek smells like cheese Cheetos," "You are worse than watered-down Aperol." And so on . . . Bad food provided relatable, funny, and effective fodder for demeaning the powers that be, making them more tangible, even edible. Lukullus, a fancy pastry store in Warsaw, decorated its Napoleon pastries with a stylized red lightning bolt, one of the symbols of the protest. The same lightning bolt appeared on top of a soup in a picture circulating on the Internet.

Why did food play such a visible role in the protests? Besides the tight connection between food and identity, which we explored in the previous chapter, the ironic jabs harped on the supposedly natural connection that, according to conservative points of view, exists between women and food. A meme started as an actual picture left on the streets of the city of Gdynia, later widely circulated on the Internet. In it, a woman in an old-fashioned housecoat is peeling potatoes. Above her, we read: "Since I am so stupid and irresponsible that I cannot make decisions about my own uterus, why is nobody afraid to eat what I cook?"

Curiously, food also made an appearance to ridicule Trump and his followers in November 2020, when the former president's supporters organized a demonstration in Washington, D.C., against the alleged election frauds that they claimed determined Joe Biden's victory. As the organizers used the #MillionMAGAMarch and #MarchForTrump hashtags to promote the initiative, actor and social media celebrity Shea Depmore asked her followers on TikTok to fill the internet with pictures of pancakes, tagging them with #MillionMAGAMarch.[2]

"That's right, Make America Pancakes Again," she wrote. "Someone please inform the K-pop stans," those same fans of Korean pop music that, a few months before, had mobilized to get hold of most tickets for a Trump rally in Tulsa, Oklahoma, so that the stadium where the event took place ended up almost empty.[3] The Internet burst with images of desserts, so that the media impact of the actual march was diluted as web searches ended up with mouthwatering sweets.

Both examples show how exclusionary gastronativism can also be found among liberals and progressives. Although the violent tones found in right-wing or xenophobic movements are absent, and the attacks are directed against the strongmen who promote forms of undemocratic nativism, protesters also took aim at these leaders' followers, often depicted as misguided or, worse, ignorant, stupid, mean, even "deplorables" (as Hillary Clinton famously described Trump's supporters in her 2016 electoral campaign). Of course, the nativist politicians' devotees level similar accusations at liberals and progressives, blamed for selling out the core values of the communities they belong to, embracing relativism, and hypocritically justifying violence when it is convenient. The debates in the U.S. about the vandalism that took place during Black Lives Matter demonstrations in the summer of 2020 and the riots at the Capitol on January 6, 2021, reflect such polarization. While it cannot be denied that these political barbs preclude any fruitful conversation about the actual motives for discontent on both sides, the two positions are not equivalent, as one group strives to maintain the legal guarantees that protect minorities and pluralism in liberal democracies while the other pushes to abolish them in the name of the "real people" or the "silent majority," all while claiming to defend freedom of speech, religion, and assembly.

FOOD AND PROTEST

Dishes or ingredients cannot be univocally identified with political positions and parties or defined as leftist or rightist, progressive or conservative. No modes of producing, cooking, or eating can be recognized as direct or natural expressions of sociopolitical stances. However, ideological connotations can be attributed to food when it becomes part of larger networks of meaning that support political ideals, strategies, and activities. In our exploration of gastronativism, we have reflected on how food is able to facilitate the construction, maintenance, and manifestation of identities. Commanding yet abstract ideas like tradition, heritage, and authenticity can be effectively translated into the tangible, edible elements, easier to grasp and experience because of their immediacy, their ubiquity in everyday live, and their emotional weight.

It is not surprising, then, that food appears in political protests—and not always as ironically as in the cases we just discussed. Public dissent can quickly turn confrontational, even violent, especially when there is not enough food around or when it is too expensive. The 2020 demonstrations were not the first in which food had made an appearance in Poland. When the socialist government tried to suddenly raise consumer goods prices in 1980, the shipyard workers in Gdańsk publicly vented their grievances and later organized a strike that eventually led to the formation of the independent workers union Solidarność. The twenty-one demands that the movement leaders wrote on plywood panels at the entrance of the shipyard included: "10. A full supply of food products for the domestic market, with exports limited to surpluses" and "11. The introduction of food coupons for meat and meat products (until the market stabilizes)." Workers were lamenting the failure of the socialist state to manage the production and distribution of food. Its scarcity, causing citizens to wait in long lines, became an important motivation for the critique of the regime which, in the past, had used its supposed capacity to provide for all citizens as a justification for its legitimacy.

Food availability and affordability remain a central political issue in many countries around the world. In the fall of 2013, due to a bad crop in Maharashtra and excessive rain in Karnataka in southern India, onions were sold at 80–82 rupees per kilo (more or less U.S. $0.70 per pound) at the greengrocer's, while the wholesale price hovered around 60 rupees (about US $0.50 per pound). In the previous five years, the wholesale price had oscillated between 25 and 45 rupees per kilo, with a sudden peak in 2008 at 55. Onions are an important ingredient in many Indian cuisines, especially considering that a sizable segment of the population is vegetarian. The price spike put a serious dent in the food budget of many poor families, raising fears of inflation. The Hindu fundamentalist BJP, then part of the opposition, used the sensitive issue to blame the government, at the time dominated by the Indian National Congress Party, of corruption and mismanagement.[4] As elections for the lower house of the national parliament were to take place after a few months, the clamor over food prices was meant to influence the less affluent voters. The BJP managed to rise to power and maintain it, but ironically the price of onions, which created unrest among farmers in 2018 and again in 2020, still haunts Prime Minister Narendra Modi's hold on power.[5]

At the end of 2020, hundreds of thousands of farmers, including many former supporters of the BJP, descended on Delhi to protest an agricultural reform that would deregulate the sector.[6] Before the proposed changes, farmers were guaranteed a minimum price for their crops through auctions at their state's Agricultural Produce Market Committees, which allowed them to plan for the following crop cycle. The reform would eliminate those minimum prices, allowing producers to sell to anybody they want, including individuals and private companies, across different market areas. It would also standardize the taxation of goods and services. Although the official motto of the reform is "one nation, one market," farmers fear that their safety nets would be eliminated to the advantage of middlemen and wholesalers. As I finish writing this book, in winter 2022, Modi promised that he would repeal the three laws constituting the reform. Although it was not clear if minimum prices for crops would be guaranteed, farmers vowed to end the protest they had organized around Delhi to maintain pressure on the government.[7]

Food has frequently played a central role in Indian politics and in mass demonstrations. One of the causes of the Indian revolt of 1857 against the British Raj was the rumor that the British Army had coated rifle cartridges with cow and pork fat, so when soldiers bit off the cartridge covering to use them, they were effectively forced to ingest an animal that was sacred for the Hindu and one that was impure for Muslims.[8] Although the colonial government vehemently denied the hearsay, that very denial was interpreted as a confirmation of the cover-up, which led whole army units to mutiny. In 1930 Mahatma Gandhi organized a march for over two hundred miles from his retreat near Ahmedabad to the Arabian Sea to protest the taxes imposed by the Raj on salt. As Indians had been prohibited from collecting or selling salt since 1882, massive crowds joined him in an act of civil disobedience that was meant to shame the British authorities for trying to control even the most basic aspect of their colonized subjects' lives.[9]

At times, political instability follows food crises that governments do not bring about. Between the end of 2007 and the spring of 2008, Port-au-Prince in Haiti, Douala in Cameroon, Maputo in Mozambique, the outskirts of Dhaka in Bangladesh, Jakarta in Indonesia, just to mention a few locations, all saw demonstrations and riots caused by sudden increases in food prices that brought daily life to a halt. In Haiti, food expenses ballooned by between 50 and 100 percent, causing the prime minister to resign under pressure from massive rallies. Overall, between March 2007 and March 2008, the world price of corn surged by 31 percent, rice 74 percent, soybeans 87 percent, and wheat a whopping 130 percent.[10] Citizens in countries where those commodities are main staples took to the streets, even when national governments had few countermeasures to offer. The price spike was caused by numerous concurrent factors outside of their control, all connected with the neoliberal mode of globalization: financialization of the commodities markets, the international financial crisis, increases in the cost of oil and other agricultural inputs, expansion of the demand for biofuels, and the dwindling national reserves of grains.[11]

FOOD AS A POLITICAL WEAPON

The international community has intervened through direct deliveries of food to areas that experience humanitarian emergencies caused by famines, war, social unrest, or natural disasters. Inevitably, food aid itself becomes a political tool. After World War II and during the Cold War, the U.S. used food aid not only as a display of goodwill but also as a reminder of its power. Its example was soon followed by Canada and Western European countries.[12] Today, most high-income countries contribute to alleviate hunger, whose elimination—or at least radical reduction—has been indicated as one of the United Nations Sustainable Development Goals, meant to be achieved by 2030.

However, at times, local actors wage their control over food aid as a political weapon. In 2011, during the Somali civil war, the Shabab Islamic militia stopped international aid from reaching the local population, which was already ravaged by draught and famine caused by the conflict. Accusing the international aid agency of political meddling, the militia condemned hundreds of thousands of people to persistent food scarcity.[13] In April 2020, Philippines president Rodrigo Duterte threatened that he would order soldiers to shoot demonstrators during the protests in Manila's Quezon City shantytown against the lack of relief supplies that had been promised at the beginning of the COVID-19 lockdown of the area.[14] These horrific events demonstrate that while food security may be a necessary component of national peace and international relations, it is far from being universally considered a human right for everybody. Inequalities in access to food are, to a certain extent, deemed inevitable, defining social stratification within individual countries and power relations on the global scene.

Such inequalities and their significance may be the reason people seem endlessly captivated by the eating habits of the rich and the powerful. Media often focus on what political candidates consume to assess their values, actions, and statements. Food ends up being observed as a window into politicians' real attitudes and personalities, and their gestures are dissected ad nauseam. U.S. politics provide great examples. In 2007, then presidential candidate Barack Obama's observation about the high price of arugula at Whole Foods, an upscale chain of U.S. supermarkets, was read as a symptom of his elitism and detachment from the life of the common people. He made that comment while in Iowa, where arugula was quite exotic and said supermarket chain was not even present.[15] New York City major

Bill de Blasio was mocked for eating pizza with a fork, which, although being a current custom in Italy, was perceived as pretentious by large sections of his electorate.[16] Politicians may go to great lengths to be seen eating ordinary fare in down-to-earth places. The reasoning behind these occurrences seems to be "If you do not eat like the people, how can you represent the people?" Former U.S. president Donald Trump frequently and proudly performed his love for fast food, presumably embracing it as a quintessential symbol, not only of what real Americans eat, but also of American ingenuity and entrepreneurship. In January 2019, he offered burgers and pizza from national chains at a formal event celebrating the Clemson Tigers, the national college football champions, in the State Dining Room of the White House.[17]

The upper classes have historically used food to showcase their dominance and assert their social status, differentiating themselves from the hoi polloi. Displays of conspicuous consumptions were common in Ancient Rome, where powerful families secured the support of political clients through carefully orchestrated invitations to lavish feasts. From the Middle Ages, in Europe it was considered an honor to be included in the exclusive banquets of royalty and nobility, and the lower classes were happy with the distribution of leftovers that often followed them. Feasts also became a favorite subject for painters, multiplying the propaganda effect of placing the powerful in an inaccessible sphere, separated from the normal people. The publication of courtly cookbooks and, later, printed reproductions of banquet scenes performed the same function. Louis XIV perfectly understood the performative power of public food consumption and the spectacles that went with them as a way to unify the nobility around his political goals. The Versailles architectural complex, with its large ballrooms and gardens, provided a perfectly stunning background to those revelries. Such fascination with the food of those in power endures, at times in critical terms, as in Roxy Paine's *Dinner of the Dictators* (1993–1995), a hyperrealistic wooden table on which the favored meals of twelve historical figures are assembled, from Genghis Khan and Napoleon to Hitler, Haile Selassie, and Papa Doc Duvalier.

FOOD AND TOTALITARIAN POLITICS

Food and food production were propaganda tools in socialist totalitarian regimes, all while causing some of the worst famines in the history of humanity.[18] Between 1928 and 1940, the Soviet Union adopted radical politics of agricultural collectivization. Joseph Stalin pursued a rural policy aimed at establishing collective (*kolkhoz*) and state (*sovkhoz*) farms to increase production of export crops, raw materials, and reliable food supplies for the industrial (and mostly urban) sectors of the country. The human and cultural impact of these policies is hard to gauge, but it is now widely accepted that they took a huge toll on large sections of the rural population. Fertile Ukraine, for instance, was struck by a tremendous famine in 1932–1933, which affected millions of people.[19] With their traditional social structures threatened and their standards of life worsening, farmers often opposed collectivization, resorting to sabotage, strikes, and destruction of property. These acts of resistance caused innumerable arrests, confinements in labor camps, and executions. Private farming plots, completely banned only at the height of collectivization, ensured the survival of the population in rural areas and the continuation of local food customs. All along, the Soviet regime continued to deny the famine.

After Mao Zedong's proclamation of the People's Republic of China on October 1, 1949, one of the first interventions of the Communist government was the redistribution of land from the landlords to the peasants. In the following years, land and farm tools were pooled into cooperatives and later into collective farms, which controlled the production, price, and distribution of products. Between 1958 and 1960, the government launched the set of policies known as the Great Leap Forward, meant to overcome the backwardness of China's economy, industry, and technology by leveraging the vast manpower of the Chinese population. To increase the agricultural output, the government created the people's communes, which marked the end of private land ownership. Farmers were often required to stop cooking in their homes and eat in collective canteens to increase efficiency in food consumption and allegiance to the ideals of the Communist party. Three years of bad harvests were compounded by requests from the authorities to melt all available metal to build industrial machineries. Agriculture faced enormous difficulties, leading to a widespread famine that lasted from 1959 to 1961 and caused incalculable numbers of victims, with rough estimates ranging between 15 and 30 million deaths.[20] Nevertheless, until his death, Mao pointed to the overall long-term reduction of hunger in China as one of the main achievements of his regime, refusing to acknowledge the devastating famine. Food would again play a crucial role in Chinese politics, starting from the late 1970s, when Deng Xiaoping introduced a series of reforms that allowed farmers to grow crops and sell them on the free market after meeting the quota assigned by central planning. It was the beginning of the Chinese economic boom.

Food was also a strategic tool of propaganda for fascist dictators of the twentieth century (Benito Mussolini in Italy, Adolf Hitler in Germany, and António de Oliveira Salazar in Portugal) who embraced the expansion of agriculture and husbandry, as well as technological advances in those fields, to bolster their control over food production in their countries and over the lives of their citizens.[21] Food was a tangible expression of those governments' power and their capacity to take care of their populations. During a campaign to increase wheat output, for example, Mussolini showed up shirtless at harvest season where he was filmed as he participated in the labor. As early as 1924, to reassure Italians about the availability of food regardless of what they were actually experiencing, the fascist government produced many documentaries focusing on the life and production of rural workers who were presented as the backbone of the country. Italian fascism also took advantage of the symbolic power of food. Bread became a focus for fascist propaganda, which prompted citizens to limit its consumption. School children were taught a small poem that Mussolini wrote in 1928 for Bread Day, a day dedicated to the appreciation of the precious food: "Love bread, heart of the home, aroma of the table, joy of the hearth. Respect bread, sweat of the brow, pride of work, poem of sacrifice. Honor bread, glory of the fields, fragrance of the earth, feast of life. Don't waste bread, wealth of the motherland, God's sweetest gift, the most sacred prize of men's toil."

The regime co-opted the simplest of food to boost the Italians' allegiance to fascism, which was already massive. How did this happen? How can political forces with specific—although shifting—values and goals manage to get large portions of whole populations behind their actions and strategies? Some suggestions may be found in political theorist Antonio Gramsci's reflection.[22] Gramsci was a journalist and a leader of the Italian Communist Party who, imprisoned by the fascist regime for most of his adult life, used his time in jail to reflect on the political and social conditions in Italy, the clutch that the Fascist Party had on its people, and the role of culture in those dynamics. Despite his Marxist background, he felt he could not dismiss everyday customs as a "superstructure" with no influence on social and political life, a mere reflection of economic structures and production relations. The meteoric rise of fascism, its enthusiastic embrace by large portions of Italians, and the alignment it generated among very different social groups, from industry leaders to World War I veterans, had to be grounded in something other than just economics. The answer Gramsci gave was that the Fascist Party had gained dominance, which he called "hegemony," in that it had created political, social, and cultural arrangements that met the interests (real or imagined) of many other social groupings, thus ensuring its dominant position in Italy.

Fascism managed to exploit the elitist attitudes of Italian intellectuals, especially the ones on the left, and their incapacity to establish lively and productive relationships with other classes, from the bourgeoisie to the proletariat. Mussolini was able to speak to the imagination, the dreams, and the material and immaterial needs of the masses, influencing their mentalities and behaviors. Due to its centrality in everyday life, food played a central role in the party's efforts. When an embargo was decreed against Italy after its attack on Ethiopia, the regime convinced Italians to embrace autarky, relying on local products and renouncing imported goods like coffee or cocoa as a patriotic sacrifice.[23] Gramsci specifically examined serial novels and opera as examples of popular entertainment: two genres that nowadays sit comfortably in the "highbrow" categories. Gramsci's reflection is still relevant today and can be extended to food, which politicians frequently turn into embodied symbols of shared ideas and values. Food can provide a common language to different segments of the population that otherwise would have different priorities, needs, and goals.

Of course, food is a double-edged sword for the powers that decide to exploit it. If the legitimacy of a regime and its political authorities is connected to the availability of food, its scarcity immediately becomes cause for discontent and, at times, rebellion, as the examples from Poland and India at the beginning of this chapters suggest. In both cases, the tight connection between food and power is undeniable, which explain its centrality in gastronativist slogans and strategies.

Food's significance in contemporary politics prompts us to reflect on modes of embodiment that bypass the discursive dimension. Culinary practices and edible material can turn into nonverbal expressions of gastronativism in ways that are public and demonstrative or alternatively, carried out in private or within small circles, often messy and not really choreographed. In fact, to be fully effective, the political use of food in gastronativism needs to carry across as spontaneous, coming from the ever-bubbling spring of the "real people," regardless of how they are defined. To be successful, it needs to be unmediated, emotional, and easy to grasp. We see a certain prevalence of apparently spur-of-the-moment demonstrations instead of planned parades; graffiti and posters instead of paintings; destruction of monuments instead of their construction or conservation; Tiktok snippets and YouTube videos instead of documentaries and feature films.

While aimed at regional or national audiences, once these social media expressions of gastronativism become viral, they are likely to inspire similar manifestations in other parts of the world. The opportunities provided by technology and the diffusion of smart phones and the Internet, however, do not completely explain the global impact of activities and strategies that are seemingly rooted in local contexts. These are able to become internationally relevant because the issues underlying them or against which they react are widespread beyond the borders within which they originate. Once again, gastronativism reveals its connections with the dynamics of neoliberal globalization that, although circumstantial and adapted to different situations, operate following similar principles and objectives. That said, the horizon in which most communities experience globalization continues to be, at least partly, national, even when it intersects with internal tensions and international events. As a consequence, the exploration of gastronativism requires engaging with ideas and behaviors connected to the nation, nationality, and patriotism, which are the topic of part 3.

PART THREE

BORDERS AND FLOWS

Chapter Five

FOOD, NATIONS, AND NATIONALISM

WHAT IS Italian cuisine? Although food lovers around the world constantly refer to it, what does it include? In 2011, on the 150th anniversary of the proclamation of Italy as a unified country after centuries of political fragmentation, the popular Italian wine and food magazine *Gambero Rosso* asked its readers precisely this question.¹ Its editors invited them to identify the most representative foods and dishes of Italian cuisine through an online survey. Parmigiano Reggiano had the highest percentage of mentions (53.5 percent), followed by extra virgin olive oil (43.8 percent), pizza Napoletana (43.2 percent), and buffalo mozzarella (40 per cent). Surprisingly, more participants appeared to consider rice (37.4 percent) to be more representative of "Italian" cuisine than bread (36.7 percent) and spaghetti (34.1 percent). The latter received the same percentage of mentions as the Christmas dessert *panettone*, a specialty from Milan that acquired national visibility (and distribution) only after

World War I, when its industrial production took off. The top fifteen items in the *Gambero Rosso* survey also included Florentine-style steak, Genovese-style pesto, lasagna, pasta *amatriciana* (a typical Roman dish with cured pork cheek *guanciale*, pecorino cheese, and tomato), mortadella, and Barolo wine.

The list does not have statistical value, as it reflected voluntary responses from the food magazine readers and, more specifically, those with online access. Among the respondents, a majority were located in the North, which skewed their preferences toward specialties from that area. At any rate, the list reveals the strong local character of the cuisines of Italy. Some products, such as pesto and buffalo mozzarella, have gained national renown in the last two or three decades and only recently have become available all around the country. Pesto varies from the homemade to the artisanal and the mass produced. What makes certain foods "Italian" is their strong connection with local identities, artisanal skills, and traditions, but the influence of production and distribution structures, as well as marketing, is evident. In fact, it may be more fitting to talk about food in Italy than Italian food. However, Italians are very quick to praise their national dishes and products when talking with foreigners, becoming defensive when they are compared with other cuisines and arguing for their protection in international trade. National pride inevitably kicks in. That said, the variety of products featured in the *Gambero Rosso* list suggests that Italian cuisines do not have a definitive canon, although one could contend that the unending consternation pineapple on pizza elicits in most Italians could be interpreted as an expression of a stable nationwide culinary identity.

Reflections about food and the nation are also taking place in Poland. The Ministry of Agriculture and Rural Development has taken on the endeavor of identifying the canon of Polish cuisine in terms of dishes, ingredients, and products. After a few informal conversations with experts including chefs, food producers, media personalities, and scholars, a first list was officially launched on August 29, 2019, at the Museum of King Jan III's Palace in Wilanów, Warsaw. The goal of the canon, as stated in the ministry's website, is to answer the question "What is Polish cuisine?" The ministry then opened a round of consultations to further develop the idea before transferring the project to the newly formed National Institute of Culture and Rural Heritage.[2] The concept of canon inevitably evokes some rigidity, pointing to the research of an "essence" of Polish cuisine neatly coinciding with its present-day borders and homogeneous demographics. In fact, a canon also implies the exclusion of what is considered not worth or fitting of an overarching principle or project. Not an easy task, due to the complex history of Poland, its partition among different empires in the nineteenth century, the Nazi and Soviet occupations, the massive relocations of entire populations after World War II, and the inclusion in the Soviet economic and political sphere until 1989.

GASTRONATIONALISM

The two cases exemplify the different approaches toward national cuisine that social scientists Atsuko Ichijo and Ronald

Ranta have described as unofficial, bottom-up and official, top-down: the former is based on practices and perceptions of consumers and producers, outside of direct interventions of governments, while the latter is mediated or promoted by national authorities through initiatives that include domestic policies and branding as well as international diplomacy and trade (as we will see in the next two chapters).[3] In the Italian case, a magazine turned to the idea of a national cuisine to celebrate a historic anniversary, but the intentions of editors and readers did not reflect nationalistic political positions beyond cultural pride. In the Polish case, the focus on cuisine as a reflection of a well-defined, stable national identity constitutes a central element in the political agenda of a conservative government that claims to be the interpreter and the defender of Polish culture and traditions against internal and external threats, all while trying to control the historical narrative of the country's past.[4]

The Italian and Polish cases constitute two very different expressions of what sociologist Michaela deSoucey qualifies as "gastronationalism," which "signals the use of food production, distribution, and consumption to demarcate and sustain the emotive power of national attachment, as well as the use of nationalist sentiments to produce and market food."[5] DeSoucey developed the concept to tease out the tension between the homogenizing power of globalization and the emergence of local identity politics based on the idea of the nation. The relations between locality and globalization are quite intricate: the former has emerged as a relevant and politically charged element precisely as a reaction to the latter. In other words, the global and the local present themselves as two aspects of the same phenomenon.[6] These processes require reexamining the role of the nation, nationalism, "gastronationalism," and the idea of the existence of national cuisines. Scholar Jason Edwards describes the latter as "contingent symbolic representations of national identity made by different people in different times and places."[7] However, Edwards clarifies, "there is no such thing in modern nation-states (perhaps with the exception of some microstates) as a distinctive national cuisine that is shared by all these members—or even a majority—of the nation."[8]

Nevertheless, food is a tangible element though which the citizens of a country imagine being part of a single, coherent body: the nation. The idea of the nation is one of the most powerful ways for a government to turn a diverse and fragmented population into a more or less unified political community with shared values and goals (including the defense of the nation itself). However, as political scientist Benedict Anderson observed, like other social formations, the nation is an "imagined community" that needs to be constantly revamped and buttressed. It is impossible for its members to actually build meaningful, direct relationships with all the other citizens.[9] Food plays a crucial role in the construction and daily reproduction of national identity through what social scientist Michael Billig has described as "banal nationalism," which mobilizes and organizes people in less formal ways than religion or state institutions.[10] Providing narratives and practices that can anchor individual and community identities, food allows authorities and governments to influence citizens through interventions in their material and physical life (Michel Foucault called these dynamics "biopolitics").[11] Individuals are transformed into members of a nation through their most mundane, everyday activities, including producing, buying, cooking, and eating food. These behaviors easily congeal into forms of bottom-up food nationalism, at times through ideas of tradition, heritage, and authenticity, that may or may not overlap or interact with the top-down initiatives of governments and authorities.

The idea of national cuisines and a hierarchy among them has enjoyed resonance since the formative period of colonial empires. From the sixteenth century, Western European powers, armed with a sense of moral and cultural superiority and the idea of the preeminence of the white race and its civilizing mission, have been practicing what has been described as ecological or biological imperialism.[12] Besides introducing new crops in their colonies to suit their cultural preferences and commercial priorities, the food of the colonized was intentionally demeaned to the advantage of the colonizers. Over time, a sense of inferiority about local food emerged among colonial subjects, whose upper strata often ended up considering European food as the pinnacle of refinement.[13] The Vietnamese in French Indochina embraced bread, so that the French baguette became the basis for the now fashionable *banh mi*.[14] West African palm wines were demeaned and often prohibited to the advantage of imported European liquors.[15] Also in West Africa, colonizers pushed farmers to prefer imported Asian rice to the indigenous varieties that provided lower yields. The new rice also replaced native grains such as fonio, which, although well adapted to the local arid conditions, was branded as backward and uncivilized.[16] As Western powers solidified into nation-states in the nineteenth century, food practices and traditions turned into tangible symbols of a country's character. Just like anthems or flags, they were easily recognizable, and ideas about national cuisine emerged that were more specific than previous references to nationality, such as *à la française* or *à la russe*, which denoted more culinary and cultural styles than states and governments.

Identifying and marking some ingredients, dishes, or customs as national inevitably generated exclusions. Such choices were also visible in cultural expressions that were not sanctioned by the government. In 1891, Pellegrino Artusi published his *La scienza in cucina e l'arte di mangiare bene* (Science in the kitchen and the art of eating well), widely considered to be the first cookbook that consciously embraced the idea of an Italian cuisine. He took on the task of presenting a set of recipes that would reflect the newly formed kingdom at a time when Italy was still an abstract concept for many who found themselves within its borders. He put together a glossary of technical terms that would allow all Italians to understand the book, chose recipes from most areas of the country (although inflecting them through his own local customs and bourgeois taste), and tackled the influence of French culinary traditions, both respected as prestigious and described as foreign. Buffalo mozzarella and pasta *amatriciana*, which ranked high in the 2011 *Gambero Rosso* list, were not even mentioned in Artusi's book, and Neapolitan pizza was, for him, a dessert with almonds, eggs, and ricotta.

BUILDING NATIONAL CUISINES

The creation of national cuisines is an ongoing process that is easily coopted in national construction or reconstruction. In

Catalonia, local actors ranging from citizens to political authorities vie for greater autonomy from the national Spanish government and cherish regional culture to nourish their sense of nation, authenticity, and heritage. However, because of the political tensions with Madrid, any reference to Catalan culinary traditions as a national cuisine is a touchy issue. Against this background, in the early 2000s, local universities and the Catalan Institute of Cuisine and Gastronomic Culture, a private foundation, launched a study of the territory that aimed at taking a snapshot of the culinary landscape as it was at that specific moment. Although led by experts, the project focused on identifying what Catalans themselves consider to be heritage and tradition, not what researchers or authorities may think. Numerous teams traveled throughout all the counties of the region, organizing focus groups and interviewing restaurant goers, housewives, cooks, and local experts. The respondents indicated the dishes they considered as part of their family customs and daily practices. For these dishes to be included in what became the Corpus of Catalan Culinary Heritage, they had to show at least a fifty-year-long history (more or less three generations) and they could not be the invention of a single family or village.[17] In order to meet the latter requirement, the dishes had to be found in at least three different locations. Through this process, around nine hundred dishes were identified, each with their local variations in ingredients and techniques. The experiment established a methodology that was meant to be applied at different intervals of time while providing a model for other regions or countries. In 2011, a first revision took place and more dishes were added, reaching a total of about eleven hundred, integrated with analysis of traditional cookbooks. A second revision is in the works. The process presents a mix of top-down and bottom-up approaches, which reflects the desire to recognize the distinctiveness of Catalan cuisine and Catalan culture while also raising its profile internationally, as Catalonia has become one of the main destination for global tourism.

In Colombia, access to foods and products from all over the country, characterized by an astonishing biological, agricultural, and ethnic diversity, is one of the most tangible effects of the process of pacification that is meant to put an end to the conflict among the government and various guerrillas and paramilitary groups. The Colombian government entered in talks with the AUC paramilitary (Autodefensas Unidas de Colombia, or United Self-Defense of Colombia) in 2003 and signed an agreement with the FARC guerrillas (Fuerzas Armadas Revolucionarias de Colombia, or Revolutionary Armed Forces of Colombia) in 2016. While the conflict and the activities of the drug cartels previously hampered communication and physical transportation of goods (including food), now it is possible for Colombians to explore the culinary richness of their country. In this spirit, in 2012, the Ministry of Culture launched the *Biblioteca Básica de Cocinas Tradicionales de Colombia*, seventeen volumes (available for free online) organized around historical and anthropological topics, as well as geographical regions, with the goal of promoting the knowledge, safeguarding, and support of traditional cuisines.[18] Although a top-down initiative, the attention to local specialties has thwarted most attempts at defining Columbian national cuisine by selecting or excluding elements. Diversity has been highlighted as one of its most valuable characteristics. The goal was not to impose a unified, coherent version of the nation, but rather to celebrate the survival of the nation itself after years of ordeals. Of course, that does not mean that inequalities and divisions based on class, ethnicity, or location have disappeared.

Like Colombia, which has seemingly embraced its stunning diversity as a way out of years of violence, Mexico and Peru have also adopted the idea of a national cuisine as an antidote to political turmoil: the apparent domination of drug cartels for the former, terrorism for the latter. As we will see in the next chapter, Mexico has emphasized its culinary heritage as "ancestral," based on locality, tradition (especially focused on the centrality of corn), and the role of women in maintaining dishes and culinary techniques.[19] However, this approach has led to sidelining ethnic cuisines that do not identify with the majoritarian mestizo culture. It has also been observed that festivals, media appearances, and restaurants have become the domain of elite professionals, often males, at the expense of women and working-class communities.[20]

Similar elite-driven efforts have been observed in Peru.[21] The country has become a fashionable place for foodies because of the richness and diversity of its traditions and the work of chefs that have "elevated" local practices to attract international attention. Elements of regional and ethnic traditions are included and celebrated. *Anticuchos*, *chanfainita*, and other specialties whose origins are widely attributed to citizens of African descent are widely appreciated. Cuisine is highlighted as a tool to favor inclusion and to eliminate racial tensions, and its celebration is meant to celebrate Peru's diversity and multiculturality. However, disadvantaged communities remain relatively invisible or relegated to second-class citizenship.[22] Critics have lamented that "the historic and contemporary contributions of marginalized groups become narrative props rather than authentic voices."[23] In other words, the prevalence of white, male chefs ends up reinforcing social and ethnic stratification.

Cultural diversity can make the definition of a national cuisine a dubious task. That is the case in India, where religious and social tensions often express themselves through food choices. Already in the late 1980s, anthropologist Arjun Appadurai observed how de facto negotiations about what Indian cuisine is resulted from demographics shifts connected to the increase of literacy, urbanization, and the rise of Anglophone commercial and professional middle classes that relocate for work not only to large metropolises but also to smaller towns.[24] Women are the main actors shaping the new approach to a national cuisine, as they are still mostly in charge, not only feeding their family but also performing status and refinement in public gatherings and private dinners.

Indian cuisines are still regional, built around local ingredients and practices and profoundly influenced by gender, class, religion, and ethnicity. The emerging national cuisine does not erase the fundamental diversity of the culinary landscape, but rather tends to make it legible and accessible across the country, at least among those with sufficient social mobility and cultural adventurousness. Its circulation takes place though cookbooks and magazines in English, as well as via TV shows, websites, and social media, which further mark its classed features. A new foodie culture has become visible in many large urban centers around the country, cosmopolitan in character and relatively inaccessible to the majority of the population. Removed from the daily lives of millions of Indians, this inherently diverse and tolerant national cuisine, which at the same time explores and glorifies regional cuisines and the uniqueness of their ingredients, does not reflect the ideological uses of food in its most violent manifestations, which we discussed in chapter 1.

Defining a national cuisine is not a challenge in India only. What dish can be acknowledged as fully "national" in such a diverse country as Nigeria, with its history marked by colonialism, the ongoing efforts at building a nation-state, and simmering tensions among its various ethnicities? Jollof rice is frequently mentioned as "the" national dish, but it is common in other West African nations, such as Senegal and Gambia, which also claim it as their own. In Nigeria, most specialties can be defined in terms of geographical or ethnic origin, and they vary enormously due to climate, natural environment, religion, and history. Government authorities, especially those in charge of culture and tourism, have underlined the importance of gastronomy for nation building and rural development.[25] Local food writers support this perspective through the Internet and books, often geared toward international markets.[26] Foreigners also take on the task of introducing and translating Nigerian food culture to outsiders, raising concerns in terms of appropriation and lack of in-depth knowledge.[27] At any rate, what recipes end up in these collections? Who decides those dishes that deserve to represent the whole country and those that are instead left out because they are too local or too backward?

Under what authority? The selections may reflect internal religious, ethnic, and class dynamics without excluding the influence of perceptions about what may be considered interesting, exciting, and worthy among global cosmopolitan gourmets.

COSMOPOLITAN CUISINES

Identifying a national cuisine can be particularly challenging in New World countries where wave after wave of migrants have settled. Conversations and debates go on in the U.S., where the descriptor *New American Cuisine* is widely used among food professionals and in the media. But such definition begs the question of what the original American cuisine was and whether one has actually ever existed. The culinary landscape of the country is the result of ongoing adaptations, hybridizations, and creolization, as well as hegemonic attempts at whitening and making the cuisine more proper. Are regional traditions, which have become the object of renewed interest, the true expressions of American food? Anthropologist Sidney Mintz controversially suggested that what most Americans actually share is not a more or less defined collection of ingredients and dishes, but rather a set of practices such as snacking on prepared and packaged foods, eating out, ordering in, and preferring a diet high in sugar, far, and salt.[28] More recently, the tensions underlying any attempt at a national cuisine have been highlighted by controversies about culinary appropriation. The accusation refers mostly to white chefs and experts, including food writers and cookbook authors, who use the culinary cultures of minority communities or communities of color to their own advantage without acknowledging their privilege in being able to do so.

The tension between traditions that are identified as local and the acceptance of immigrant foods can lead to two different approaches to defining a national cuisine. The one often found in exclusionary gastronativism focuses on identifying original elements and practices widely attributed to an authentic, home-grown culture, at times with parochial undertones. The cosmopolitan one, frequently present in nonexclusionary forms of gastronativism, not only matter-of-factly acknowledges migrants' contributions to the food scene but also highlights them as an expression of a country's openness and multiculturality. In 2001, Foreign Secretary Robin Cook famously pointed to chicken tikka masala as a UK national dish in a talk about the relationship between Britishness and multiculturality. Chicken tikka masala's popularity and widespread consumption were not the only motivations for the politician's statement. For him, it was "a perfect illustration of the way Britain absorbs and adapts external influences. Chicken Tikka is an Indian dish. The Massala [sic] sauce was added to satisfy the desire of British people to have their meat served in gravy."[29] Against this celebration of hybridization, frequently stigmatized by Brexit supporters as one of the causes of the UK's perceived economic and cultural decadence, some circles have elevated roast beef to a symbol of the nation, especially after the controversies around the mad cow crisis in the late 1980s.

Whatever the processes and the political worldviews behind the elaboration and definition of a national cuisine may be within a country's borders, they are unsurprisingly entangled in global dynamics. These include the legacy of colonialism, the tensions of decolonization, geopolitical conflicts, and migration fluxes. With the complicity of borderless social media, the cultural imperialism of gourmet cosmopolitanism increasingly determines what is valuable and trendy. Such complexity lends itself to exploitation in gastronativist projects that extend their reach to the international stage of diplomacy and trade disputes, as we will see in the next two chapters.

Chapter Six

FOOD AND DIPLOMACY

THE SPACIOUS ground-floor space in the former residence of the ambassador of Spain in Washington, D.C., was packed with people. All around the walls, large, colorful, artistic pictures of Spanish ingredients and specialties revealed what the event was all about: Spanish food. The audience was composed of professionals and enthusiasts that had come to hear a panel discussion about *jamón* (Spanish ham), widely appreciated and made even more visible by the global fame of Spain's renowned chefs. The fame of the products also grew thanks to the popularity of Spanish restaurants, especially those inspired by tapas: small bite-size portions that make a meal varied and fun, while allowing customers to have more control on how much they eat and spend. On the panel with me were a U.S. food scholar and jamón producers from Spain. As a food expert, and as an Italian, I found myself in the position of discussing a delicacy that is often considered a close competitor of various kinds of prosciutto from Italy. Personally, I like them both, as they are quite different, but during the jamón tasting, which followed the panel discussion, members of the audience approached me to elicit reactions about the supposedly heated rivalry, assuming some sort of built-in gastronationalism.

The occasion was part of a series called Eat Spain Up, which its main organizers, Gloria and Luis Miguel Rodriguez, considered as a form of cultural diplomacy to introduce Spain to foreign audiences and consumers and to stoke interest in it. Started in 2013, the series was meant to fill a void in the official communication about Spanish culinary culture, which often highlights chefs with little reference to what people do in their everyday lives. At the time, Spain was at the worst of its economic crisis, so the first challenge for the Rodriguezes was to figure out what the funding sources could potentially be, how private and public entities could collaborate, and what they might contribute toward shared economic goals such as tourism and food exports. With a grant from the Ministry of Culture, the organizers found themselves interacting with travel and trade offices as well as the authorities of the regions into which Spain is administratively divided. Between 2014 through 2017, events took place in Stockholm, Oslo, New York City, and Washington, D.C., every year in a different city, with the participation of various regions and food producers. The events did not have a fixed format, but rather responded to the needs of particular audiences and partners. They included master classes for culinary students and professional chefs, round tables, exhibitions, as well as screenings of films and documentaries about Spanish food.

Making different regional entities—from tourism to agriculture offices—work collaboratively was difficult, as bureaucratic areas are still very compartmentalized. Some of the Spanish regions were keen on the modern aspects of culinary culture; others instead wanted to showcase traditions, which they thought could better increase exports. Some stakeholders aimed at introducing products that were not yet circulating in foreign locations, while others preferred to increase the visibility of already available products.

GASTRODIPLOMACY

Eat Spain Up is a perfect example of the motivations, tensions, and dynamics behind the public-private undertakings known as *gastrodiplomacy*, a term first used in 2002 in the *Economist* magazine to describe the "Global Thai" initiative. The Thai government launched it in 2002 with the goal of increasing the number of Thai restaurants around the world from fifty-five hundred to eight thousand. The initiative would have made it easier for both Thai and non-Thai restaurateurs to import food from Thailand, hire Thai cooks, and even get soft loans.[1] The Thai government was intent on offering a positive image, possibly to counterbalance the negative perception caused by sex tourism. The label "Thai Select" was established to certify restaurants that employed Thai cooks and staff, included Thai dishes on their menus, and used imported ingredients and tableware from Thailand. In fact, agreements with foreign countries were signed to make it easier for Thai chefs to obtain work visas.

Many countries have embraced similar strategies. In 2009, the Ministry of Food, Agriculture, Forestry, and Fishery and the Ministry of Culture, Sports, and Tourism of South Korea launched the "Korean Cuisine to the World" campaign through the newly founded Korean Food Foundation. The government, with the support of private companies, believed that Korean food (or *hansik*) could ride the wave of interest in Korean culture that followed the success of its TV dramas, films, and, above all, K-pop. Besides organizing culinary events around the world (I happened to be invited to one about *soju*, the national spirit), the campaign tried to promote Korean celebrity chefs and the gastronomic style of the Joseon dynasty royal court (fourteenth through nineteenth centuries). Embracing a certain cultural conservativism, the promoters deemed this historical approach to cuisine especially dignified, lofty, and refined, perfect to counterbalance the relatively recent culinary changes brought about by the Japanese occupation and the Korean War. Moreover, South Korea zeroed in on kimchi as a winning product, thanks to its touted health benefits, its appeal as a natural product, the genuineness of its ingredients, and the centrality of traditional skills in its making. The World Institute of Kimchi was inaugurated in 2010.

The term *gastrodiplomacy* has been used to designate global campaigns of soft diplomacy meant to increase the interest in a country's gastronomy and products in order to raise its profile, generate goodwill, and enjoy economic and commercial windfalls. Gastrodiplomacy has been variously described as a "government's practice of exporting its national culinary heritage as part of a public diplomacy effort,"[2] "the practice of sharing a country's cultural heritage through food,"[3] or more simply as "winning the hearts and mind through stomachs."[4]

Although it has recently arrived at global diffusion, gastrodiplomacy is not totally new. Food has historically played an important role in official encounters, negotiations, and cultural exchanges among nations. Winston Churchill considered "tabletop diplomacy" a central tool in showing off power and influence in discussions with international decision makers.[5] Richard Nixon's 1972 dinner with Prime Minister Zhou Enlai, during which the U.S. president famously ate with chopsticks, was as significant as the better-known ping-pong-diplomacy in the establishment of relations between the U.S. and the People's Republic of China.[6]

Conversely, food can cause diplomatic embarrassment. Queen Elizabeth visited Belize in 1985 at a time when the country, which had gained its independence from the UK in 1981, felt threatened by neighboring Guatemala. The meal included roasted gibnut, a nocturnal rodent the locals consider a delicacy. While the queen diplomatically praised the chef, the British tabloids had a field day proclaiming that the sovereign had been fed "rat," causing Belizeans to accuse the UK press of racism and insensitivity. Needless to say, the gibnut suddenly acquired higher status and greater symbolic meaning in the Central American country.[7]

Former president Donald Trump's dislike for vegetables created awkward moments during his official visit to India in February 2020. On the occasion of the banquet at the Rashtrapati Bhavan, the official residence of the president of India, the palace chefs prepared a menu that was designed to please him.

Atlantic salmon was served as fish tikkas with cajun spices instead of a garam masala, and goat meat replaced Trump's beloved beef, but the efforts were not particularly appreciated.[8] During the U.S. president's visit to Gandhi Ashram in Ahmedabad, celebrity chef Suresh Khanna stuffed samosa with broccoli and corn instead of potatoes and peas, causing consternation among Indian gourmets, but apparently neither President Trump nor the First Lady tried anything from the specially designed vegetarian menu.[9]

CULINARY DIPLOMACY AND MIDSIZE COUNTRIES

The growing number of gastrodiplomacy initiatives suggests that the value of food in diplomatic relations has become evident to many governments besides its advantage in entertaining foreign guests. National authorities can use it to make a country more visible in an international landscape where food enthusiasts and professionals are increasingly interested in uniqueness, originality, and authenticity, partly as a reaction to the uniformity that many feel comes with globalization. Culinary diplomacy campaigns are particularly interesting to midsize countries that, due to their history or their limited political or economic power, would otherwise have a hard time getting themselves noticed on the global scene. Food is supposed to allow such countries to improve the way international audiences perceive them. The marketing practice of branding is applied to international relations, with the goal of making a country stand out through easily recognizable features. The targets of such strategies are not only governments but also foreign consumers, trade operators, and investors.

The emergence of gastrodiplomacy initiatives is, in itself, a direct consequence of food globalization, which allows ingredients, products, ideas, and culinary professionals to effortlessly circulate around the world. Heavily relying on social media and the Internet, current gastrodiplomacy is particularly geared toward cosmopolitan foodies that share common values and taste categories across borders, have the financial means and the interest to buy imported products, and can travel abroad. Gastrodiplomacy can also contribute to create a sense of unity and national pride around food inside the countries that engage in it. It can ideologically leverage nostalgia to smooth out domestic tensions, harkening back to the good old times before modernity and globalization.

It is difficult to gauge gastrodiplomacy's outcomes, both internally and abroad, as a variety of factors and sociopolitical processes affect the participation and collaboration of the variety of stakeholders that are necessary to secure its success. Those who hold exclusionary gastronativist positions may well patronize Chinese restaurants, Mexican taco stands, or kebab stores, quite ubiquitous in many countries, on a regular basis, but they are likely to be uninterested in knowing more about the culture these foods come from or in even considering them as traditions worth exploring, apart from their accessibility and affordability. Lesser-known culinary traditions may not even appear on their radar, also due to the limited numbers or relative political invisibility of the immigrants who are connected with them.

This is the case for many midsize countries such as Thailand, Korea, and Peru. Gastrodiplomacy tends, then, to remain an elite phenomenon, unlikely to counteract exclusionary gastronativism and disconnected overall from the goals and strategies of nonexclusionary gastronativism.

CULINARY TOURISM

Gastrodiplomacy is also connected with culinary tourism, as in the case of Taiwan. In 2010, its Ministry of Economic Affairs and the Tourism Bureau inaugurated a promotional campaign to present the country as an alternative travel destination for Chinese food lovers, one with unique features determined by its colonial history and the presence of non-Chinese ethnic minorities. The government supported efforts to organize events abroad, to establish a food foundation, and to expand the global popularity of bubble tea, while private restaurant chains continued their work to indirectly promote Taiwanese food. The case of Taiwan is particularly interesting because its very nationhood is put into question by the People's Republic of China and the identification of most of its population as ethnic Chinese. The country turned to tourism as a nonconfrontational way to assert itself, taking advantage of opportunities afforded by the globalized culinary cosmopolitanism while resisting its more homogenizing aspects.

Other countries have focused on their restaurant sector, the fame of their chefs, and the uniqueness of their cuisines to attract well-off tourists. In very different ways, that is the case for Peru and Denmark, whose booming culinary scenes appeal to foodies well beyond their borders. Besides applying (so far without success) for the inclusion of its cuisine in the UNESCO list of Intangible Cultural Heritage (more about that later), the Peruvian government, together with public and private agencies, have supported the promotion of its national gastronomy abroad through the creation of a specific brand (Marca Perú), international events, films, documentaries, and even a bus trip of the most renowned chefs to Peru, Nebraska, duly recorded in a charming video.[10] Besides promoting the Peru brand and increasing citizens' pride in their own nation, the focus on cuisine is supposed to provide opportunities for economic and social advancement, especially for the historically less developed areas of the Andes and the Amazon basin.[11] Ingredients and food producers are expected to acquire prominence through the work of the chefs, which, however, tends to flourish in urban environments.

In Denmark, the idea of the New Nordic Cuisine propelled chefs onto the international scene. Local ingredients, dishes, and practices that were on the brink of extinction were brought back, wrapped in discourses of authenticity, sustainability, and creativity to which both the national and global media were sensitive. The approach was not exclusively limited to Denmark, but the country has been able to build on the notoriety of its chefs and restaurants to acquire a relevance unthinkable until recently, becoming a destination for gourmets from all over the world. In both the Peruvian and Danish cases, the success of national chefs is a reflection of their participation in relationships, collaborations, and practices that influence prevailing global standards, as reflected, for example, in the San Pellegrino World's 50 Best Restaurants list. The chefs know each other, organize activities together, and participate in events that favor both their personal brand and the country they find themselves representing. National cuisines become globally relevant when they manage to balance enough uniqueness and authenticity to offer an alternative to the uniformity of globalization and enough compliance to meet the global standards of cosmopolitan foodies. In culinary tourism, national cuisines may appear in versions that exclusionary gastronativism resents as too intellectual, expensive, and elitist and that nonexclusionary gastronativism critiques as erasing or ignoring social and ethnic rifts.

UNESCO AND INTANGIBLE CULTURAL HERITAGE

In recent years, a new international arena to showcase national cuisines as a form of gastrodiplomacy has emerged. Following requests from countries that wanted their culinary customs recognized and appreciated, the United Nations Educational, Scientific, and Cultural Organization (UNESCO) has expanded an already existing category, the Intangible Cultural Heritage, to include agricultural practices, food production, and gastronomic traditions that are place-specific and derive their value from the unique connections between communities, their material lives, and their environments.

Intangible Cultural Heritage focuses on production, preparation, and consumption of food and on how a community thinks and talks about it. While the element of intergenerational transmission is the most important, change is considered an inseparable feature of this kind of heritage. To qualify for the UNESCO list, heritage must be a living expression of the embodied experience of a community. Practices, knowledge, and skills are not meant to be frozen in time or converted into museum pieces: they are supposed to be constantly evolving to respond to new situations. What counts is a shared sense of identity and continuity that gives each community the right to determine their own heritage. According to the UN organization, the recognition of a community should not promote intolerance and discrimination against outsiders; it should rather encourage respect and dialogue through intercultural communication.

Inclusion of a culinary tradition in the Intangible Cultural Heritage list does not imply its superiority over others, but works rather as an identity marker, since it promotes appreciation for a community's culture, which can bolster its members' sense of belonging and pride as well as their engagement in keeping those practices alive. At times, the recognition reignites the interest of a community in its own products, which may have been considered plain, unexciting, or even backward. It has the potential to improve a country's international status and its visibility on the global stage. Inclusion in the UNESCO list also offers indirect economic advantages for tourism (gastronomic routes, events, infrastructure improvements) and product marketing, which is, however, explicitly forbidden by UNESCO.

As UNESCO is an intergovernmental organization, national authorities are in charge of applying for inclusion in the

Intangible Cultural Heritage list. Such top-down initiatives, which can be considered a form of international diplomacy, require executive decisions that follow political negotiations among numerous stakeholders, each with different interests, priorities, and access to power. Such debates can be used to strengthen specific viewpoints regarding what counts as the nation and what gets set aside or forgotten. The temptation of imposing a single viewpoint over all others is always present, especially because foreign audiences are among the main targets. For this reason, it is particularly important to gauge the modes of operation and the effectiveness of this approach, although data is still limited due to its relatively short history.

The first three food-related traditions were inscribed in the UNESCO list of Intangible Cultural Heritage in 2010: the gastronomic meal of the French; the Mediterranean diet (proposed by Italy, Spain, Morocco, and Greece, later joined by Cyprus, Portugal, and Croatia); and traditional Mexican cuisine ("ancient, continuous community culture, the Michoacán paradigm"). The list has been growing since then. The most recent additions in 2020 include Malta's il-Ftira ("culinary art and culture of flattened sourdough bread"); the "knowledge, know-how and practices pertaining to the production and consumption of couscous" in Algeria, Mauritania, Morocco, and Tunisia; tree beekeeping culture in Poland and Belarus; as well as Singapore's hawker culture ("community dining and culinary practices in a multicultural urban context"). Besides highlighting one of the most popular features in the dining scene of the tiny island state and a great tourist attraction, inclusion of the hawker's culture also addresses Singapore's ethnic diversity, as

Chinese, Malay, and Indians all participate in such practices, although in different ways.

The year 2013 was particularly interesting. That year, the traditional dietary cultures of the Japanese (*washoku*) were included in the UNESCO list. The inscription focused, in particular, on the new year celebrations with their consumption of rice, fish, edible plants, and other local fresh ingredients that are supposed to reflect Japan's traditional and sustainable use of natural resources. Critics have expressed doubts about how the dossier was constructed. Scholar Eric Roth noted: "The vague definition . . . from Japan's Ministry of Agriculture and other official agencies . . . does not at all resemble either what most people once ate or what they consume today. Washoku is instead an idealized dietary lifestyle, focusing on food popularized from the 1960s onwards meant to impress audiences outside Japan and guide domestic eating habits."[12] By presenting romanticized versions of what people actually do, inscriptions in the UNESCO list can function externally as forms of gastrodiplomacy and internally as ideological calls to embrace specific, and at times conservative, versions of national identity.

Also in 2013, South Korea succeeded in having *kimjang*, the making and sharing of kimchi, added to the UNESCO list. However, kimchi is produced all over the Korean peninsula. The political sensitiveness of the issue led the UN organization to also include the tradition of kimchi making in the Democratic People's Republic of Korea on the list. As part of the South Korea's gastrodiplomacy initiatives, the inscription not only reaffirmed the centrality of kimchi for national identity but also provided a cultural justification for the country's commercial claims on the product. The commercialization of similarly fermented cabbage from China and Japan, which is consumed in great quantities in South Korea, made the inscription more urgent. Trade disputes over kimchi resurfaced in 2012 when South Korea lobbied the UN Codex Alimentarius commission, which establishes internationally recognized standards and codes of conduct concerning food production and food safety, to change the English name of the main kimchi ingredient from "Chinese cabbage" (as originally described in the original 2001 definition) to "kimchi cabbage."[13] However, the current standard, amended in 2017, still features "Chinese cabbage."[14] In 2020, China, in turn, lobbied the International Organization for Standardization (ISO) to acknowledge *paocai* (salted fermented vegetables), a name that can also refer to kimchi, arousing concerns in South Korea.[15] With the goal of defending national interests and supporting their country's claims, both Korean and Chinese authorities referred to fields of knowledge ranging from culture and tradition to food technology and scientific standards. Kimchi is just an example of how political debates with strong gastronativist undertones develop in international diplomacy. In such cases, decisions are made by transnational—and supposedly neutral—organizations by applying rules that enforce and normalize the principles and practices of neoliberal globalization. As we will see in the following chapter, much as gastrodiplomacy tries to smooth over geopolitical tensions, trade issues tend to resurface. They often cause rifts that supply fodder for gastronativist controversies, both internally and internationally.

Chapter Seven

NATIONAL PRODUCTS IN THE GLOBAL MARKET

AT THE end of 2007, when people started feeling sick after eating pot stickers (*gyoza*), panic spread in Japan. Within a short period of time, it became clear that the culprits were frozen gyoza imported from China. A disgruntled employee had poisoned them with methamidophos, a banned pesticide, to protest the horrible work conditions in his company, Tianyang.[1] Although only ten people were hospitalized, the media frenzy was amplified by the upcoming Beijing Olympics and by the attempts of then prime minister Fukuda Yasuo to minimize the events and maintain commercial exchanges with China. Several factors contributed to fuel the outrage around this case: the historically complicated relations with China; the widespread perception among the Japanese that Chinese workers are uneducated, careless, and unreliable, especially regarding food safety and hygiene; the awareness that China is fundamental for Japan's food security, as the country does not produce enough food to ensure self-sufficiency; and the anxiety provoked by the inevitable integration of Japan into global trade, with all the vulnerabilities open markets bring with them. It was not surprising that exclusionary gastronativist discourse and strategies shaped the public debates that followed.

China was involved in various food-related scandals in 2008, which caused the controversies about the gyoza incidents to last for months. Large quantities of milk and infant formula were contaminated with melamine, whose nitrogen was meant to fake a higher protein content in the products. Sixteen babies were diagnosed with kidney stones. Two among those found responsible were put to death and three were imprisoned for life. Various countries stopped importing dairy products from China, and Chinese nationals scrambled to buy baby formula from abroad.[2] That same year, melamine was detected in eggs, as the substance had been added to animal feed.[3] Some tainted milk was found in Taiwan, triggering calls to ban products from China. The incident threw a negative light on the Cross-Straight Service Trade Agreement, which was being negotiated at the time to liberalize exchange of services between China and Taiwan, including food-related ones.[4] Food safety and the gastronativist discourse that emerged around it in Taiwan were sucked into broader civic debates about the country's autonomy and its position on the international stage. The episode increased the diffidence of Taiwanese consumers toward their powerful neighbor, which on the one hand is an important commercial partner and a source of food, as the local agricultural sector is shrinking, but on the other hand is a threat to the national security and independence of the island.

The Japanese companies that imported, distributed, and sold the Chinese products were stigmatized, and the government's failure at better controlling food imports was widely criticized. Japanese diets are increasingly globalized, and have been for more than a century: the adoption of foreign eating customs was part of the Meiji emperor's plan to modernize the country at the end of the nineteenth century.[5] Younger generations have embraced foreign dishes and modes of consumption.[6] In fact, gyozas became popular in Japan when formers soldiers stationed in China returned home after World War II. Nevertheless, during the scandal, many consumers took refuge in the nostalgic idea that domestic products (*kokusan*) are inherently superior and should be protected with tariffs and subsidies, that Japanese farmers are more conscientious, and that Japanese agricultural soil should be safeguarded against the expansion of real estate and industrial constructions. In the fight for the health of the nation, schools were blasted for serving imported frozen food to children, a result of budgetary necessity. Women were often portrayed as being responsible for what their families eat, as if the domestic table was the last line of defense against the nefarious effects of globalization.[7] Domestic products are not only much more expensive than imported ones, but they require more time and care in terms of preparation compared with the frozen ones coming from abroad.

However, dangers can also come from inside. While Chinese food is, at times, sold as Japanese, amplifying consumers' concerns about fraud, the earthquake, the tsunami, and the Fukushima meltdown in 2011 have intensified fears of contamination of local products. Attacks on food safety took place at the hand of Japanese nationals: toward the end of 2013, a resentful employee poisoned some products from the company Aqlifoods with the pesticide malathion. However, the case was presented as the act of an isolated criminal rather than the consequence of Japan's opening to the world, and it received much less media coverage.[8]

As a result of the 2007–8 gyoza case, imports of Chinese frozen food to Japan never went back to pre-2008 levels, and the government established the Consumer Affairs Agency to ensure consumer protection. The case suggests that the role of the national government became a central element in the Tianyang gyoza controversies because it was perceived as a protection against the external dangers inherent in international trade. Authorities are also supposed to mitigate the risks that result from the project of modernization and the technological advances Japan is so proud of. Although Japan became a world power thanks to its internationalization and participation in the global market, citizens are quick to point to globalization as the ultimate culprit for their current woes, against which governments, firms, schools, families, and individuals seem increasingly less able to intervene. The high quality of domestic food is meant to reassure the Japanese over the hazards penetration of globalization into the intimate dimensions of the individual body and domestic life can cause. The nation becomes a bulwark against the dangers that derive from lowering defenses against the worldwide circulation of goods, people, ideas, and technologies. Exclusionary gastronativists that decry the risks of foreign food end up supporting strategies and interventions that also resonate among those who embrace forms of nonexclusionary gastronativism, including local food activists and the antiglobalization movement.

TRADE AND GASTRONATIVISM

The events in Japan and Taiwan indicate the relevance that gastronativist attitudes may acquire in international trade relations. Obviously, the connection of gastronativist debates with commercial issues are not exclusive to East Asia. On October 13, 2019, the main title on the front page of *Libero*, a daily paper connected to the Italian center-right political area, proclaimed: "Food Alert: Foreign Food is Toxic. Fish, mussels, pistachios, chicken: every day a scandal at the table and in 83% of cases it is the fault of foreign products." The solution reportedly proposed by Coldiretti, the national association of small farmers? "A million of signatures to save made-in-Italy products from EU laws." The article also stigmatized French mackerel, Spanish mussels, Hungarian and Polish meat, and American almonds. Products from Spain and France constituted the gravest threat, due to their sheer quantity and the limited inspections they are subject to. According to the author of the article, this lack of control was in contrast with the strict checks and quarantines that exports from Italy have to go through.[9]

This form of exclusionary gastronativism can take extreme, at times ridiculous, forms. In December 2019, Matteo Salvini, the former Italian prime minister and leader of the anti-immigration Lega party, declared he would no longer consume the popular chocolate spread Nutella because it contained hazelnuts from

Turkey.[10] It was immediately pointed out that Italy does not produce enough hazelnuts to satisfy the demand from Nutella manufacturing. Two months later, at the European Parliament, a member of the same Lega Party brandished and threw on the floor a large Turkish chocolate bar, which the government of that country had previously distributed as a symbol of goodwill in its campaign to join the EU.[11] In both cases, the EU was faulted for limiting the political freedom and trade choices of its members.

In these politicians' opinions, the EU authorities are not invested in defending Italy's interests, which is part of the Union as much as some of the supposed culprits are. The discontent toward Brussels and its bureaucrats is not a unique Italian issue. In 2009, French and Belgian dairy producers organized demonstrations during which they gave away milk in large cities or poured it on the streets to protest the increase of EU-imposed quotas, which had lowered milk prices.[12] In 2016, farmers blocked roads in several regions of France to force the EU to rethink the trade sanctions it established against Russia after the Crimea annexation.[13] The limitations imposed on trade toward Russia had caused steep drops in the prices of milk, butter, and pork, which could not be remedied by the aid package the French government put together, as farmers deemed it insufficient.

While focusing on trade issues, the cases from Japan, Taiwan, and Italy all express a sense of besiegement: dangerous foreign matter is penetrating a safe space that nations put a lot of effort in controlling (more about that in chapter 9). The emergency clearly demarcates "us" against "them." Food not only treacherously passes national borders but also pollutes both the body politic of the nation and the physical bodies of its citizens. However, the borders and the community in question can shift over time, depending on the situation. The nation may be featured recognizably in these discourses and strategies, but while proclamations and concrete actions tend to be local, the general framework of reference is increasingly global.

The nation is purposely propped up as an ideological tool, with the result that deep structures and systemic dynamics that are transnational are hidden. After World War II and the process of decolonization that followed, nation-states remained the most visible actors in global relations but shifted toward greater coordination through international agreements. The General Agreement on Tariffs and Trade (GATT), established in 1947, eventually gave way in 1995 to the World Trade Organization (WTO), which expanded the purview of trade to services, intellectual property, finance, and even food safety.

What is at stake here are not only matters of international trade, comparative advantage, or even economic protectionism. The political debates that food-related incidents provoked in Japan, Taiwan, and Italy suggest that those concerns are accompanied and supported by deeper fears regarding the survival of one's community. If the nation is the immediate horizon for the perceived threat, its ultimate cause lies in something broader, less easy to understand, and definitely tougher to keep at bay: the unregulated dynamics of globalization, which, on the one hand, facilitate exports and is supposed to endure food security but, on the other, force countries to partly give up their protections, their internal policies, and their autonomy.

Unsurprisingly, these tensions fully expressed themselves through the fears of contagion and contamination that came to the forefront during the COVID-19 pandemic. China reacted to Australia's request for clarification on the genesis of the virus by threatening to reduce beef imports and to impose 80 percent tariffs on imported Australian barley.[14] Russia decreed an embargo on exports of wheat, barley, and corn, hoping to limit the rise in domestic prices.[15] Many agricultural businesses that employ immigrant labor (both legally and illegally) suffered from the border closures caused by the pandemic. To remedy this, special agreements were signed between national governments: for example, limited numbers of Romanian immigrants were flown to Germany to take care of the fruit and vegetable harvest.[16] In Poland, farmers asked the government to relax border restrictions to allow Ukrainian seasonal labor in; this easing also permitted Polish workers to find employment in German agriculture, which offers higher wages than they would get at home.[17]

GASTRONATIVISM, TRADE WARS, AND RURAL POLITICS

Exclusionary gastronativism has become particularly visible in the last decade, amplified by the worldwide resurgence of populism and nationalism. The leaders of these political movements are uncannily able to obtain the support of large segments of citizens, including those whose material interests and goals would appear to clash with gastronativist agendas. Agriculture provides great examples, as it is a core component of any country's food system and food culture. Import tariffs that make foreign products more expensive are generally welcome among domestic producers, even if they eventually hurt consumers. However, farmers have, at times, backed leaders whose policies, ranging from protectionism to trade wars, actually damage their own business.

Economists have been pointing out for decades that tariffs and trade wars are ultimately detrimental. To make their point, they often refer to the infamous Smoot-Hawley Tariff Act of 1930, which had an enormously negative impact on the Great Depression. In 1928, wool farmers and sugar producers asked for federal protection for their goods, which were threatened by foreign imports. Immediately, other agricultural sectors such as corn, buckwheat, and eggs, together with nonagricultural industries, also clamored to be included in the list of tariffs, even if they did not actually have any significant foreign competition. The measure caused a huge chain reaction around the world, with other countries retaliating by imposing counter tariffs. For instance, Canada increased tariffs on eggs, limiting U.S. exports to its northern neighbor, the largest market for American producers at the time.

When, in 2018, the former U.S. president Donald Trump imposed tariffs on several Chinese products, Beijing retaliated with over $30 billion worth of tariffs on imports from the U.S., which included agricultural products such as soybeans, rice, pork, and dairy.[18] It was clear that the Chinese government was trying to target goods from areas of the country where Trump enjoyed great popularity among farmers. Despite the economic consequences, many farmers maintained their support for Trump's trade wars.[19] Political rhetoric regarding the Chinese menace played a crucial role in convincing farmers to embrace Trump's approach and to consider gastronativist strategies a valid and effective response to urgent threats that originated both inside and outside the country. As other segments of society, farmers have been primed to consider the immediate problems they face as symptoms of broader dynamics explicitly connected with globalization and a circulation of goods and money that bypass rural communities. Geopolitical and nationalistic concerns are compounded by a sense of exclusion from the cultural and social changes brought about by globalization to the advantage of the urban, educated, and cosmopolitan elites. Furthermore, religion and racial identifications are easily activated to reinforce the support for trade wars in U.S. rural environments.

Around the world, rural priorities may be embraced by national governments when farmers constitute an important voting bloc or are able to cause enough trouble. The COVID-19 pandemic, putting a brake on the global movement of goods and workers, caused a temporary downturn in exports that resulted in excess production in some countries and fear of scarcity in others. During the spring of 2020, the French government invited its countrymen to eat more cheese and to use the hashtag #fromagissons (let's act for cheese) in their social media posts.[20] Belgian citizens were prompted to consume more fries to support local production of potatoes,[21] and Britons were invited to organize steak nights to maintain a sufficient level of meat consumption.[22] The Polish government published a list of "unpatriotic" dairy farms that imported milk from other countries.[23]

Even in the absence of emergencies, some farmers may reckon that, in the long term, isolationist measures will bear fruit and bolster national agriculture, even if they temporarily hurt them. Others are ready for their bottom line to take a hit in the name of patriotism or nationalism. Yet others prioritize the cultural and social values that political leaders promote over their immediate financial concerns: they see themselves as making hard but inevitable choices in a vital battle for the soul of the nation. Of course, farmers are not a monolithic block: bigger farmers can absorb momentary losses to profit from long-term gains, while smaller farmers understandably have less wiggle room to wait for things to get better. In the case of the U.S., large farmers are also better at lobbying politicians in order to obtain various forms of relief.[24] Race and ethnicity identifications may contribute to such differences: farmers belonging to minorities or disadvantaged groups tend to have different priorities, concerns, and lobbying power.[25]

Farmers who embrace ideals of self-reliance and national pride are more likely to soldier through trade wars, inefficient food safety policies, lopsided taxation and financial structures, lack of environmental protection, and overall mismanagement of water and other natural resources. Political leaders may reward farmers' political support with temporary subsidies and emergency aid that, though distorting in the long run, are saluted as signs of the leaders' care.[26] Farmers' loyalties fluster political opponents, who often are not able to explain how and why rational actors would make decisions against their own interest. The example of the impact of gastronativism in rural areas shows that material and economic factors are tightly intertwined with cultural, social, and political ones and need to be addressed in ways that take all these components into consideration. Exploiting the emotional relevance of food, politicians are able to capture the loyalty of whole economic sectors, even when these are likely to suffer from the translation of gastronativist discourse into actual taxation, finance, and trade policies.

While trade wars have been a mainstay of human history, their intensity, swiftness, and visibility have grown enormously in recent decades. Whereas some countries have profited, others, mostly low-income ones, have suffered from the policies and regulations that the new trade order has imposed on them through the WTO. At present, the international organization is at an impasse; one of the motives of contention is precisely its failure to address the needs and demands of low- and middle-income countries that, back in the 1990s, were not in any position to refuse the compromises necessary for their accession to it.[27] Built around the idea of free trade and "small" governments, neoliberal globalization allows products to circulate freely. While commodity crops like wheat, rice, or corn are marketed internationally according to broad categories based on recognizable traits, regardless of their provenance, other products acquire higher value precisely because they are connected with specific places of origin. Once again, globalization and the appreciation of the local appear to be two sides of the same phenomenon. For this reason, trade wars can whip up gastronativist passions when they are waged to fend off the homogenizing tentacles of globalization and to nurture local specificities, defending communities from the invasion of foreign, dangerous elements that can dilute their essence and their spirit. Politicians can find support for trade wars when they are supposed to protect rural productions from the penetration of cheaper, foreign commodities, often at the hand of transnational corporations. The arguments that underlie these strategies and the language that articulates them echo those that are used to oppose the presence and significance of migrants and their food, an increasingly hot topic in gastronativist debates and the focus of part 3.

PART FOUR

BETWEEN HERE AND THERE

Chapter Eight

MIGRANT FOOD

IT WAS already clear by the mid-1990s, regardless of how vocally the French declared their passion and pride for their local products and their national cuisine in all its versions, from haute cuisine to *cuisine de bistrot* and *cuisine de pays*, that couscous had become one of their favorite dishes.[1] This realization caused some cognitive dissonance: introduced into France by North African immigrants from the former colonies of Algeria, Tunisia, and Morocco, couscous reminded the French of the not so savory imperialistic phase of their history, which is still reflected in cultural anxieties and social inequalities among French citizens of various lines of descent. Nevertheless, there it was, ubiquitous in takeaway *traiteurs*, school dining halls, restaurants of all levels, and on domestic tables. To this day, it remains an open question whether the embrace of couscous is to be considered the consequence of the successful integration of migrants or rather a case of appropriation through countless adaptations. In

2007, the movie *La Grain et le moulet* (The Secret of the Grain) raised the issue again: the story of a North African family that tries to open a couscous restaurant on a boat in the southern port of Marseille displayed the underlying tensions that still exist between migrant communities, even of second or third generation, and the rest of the population. These conflicts have become even more acute after several attacks by Muslim fundamentalists in large French cities. Yet couscous is everywhere, still recognized as a dish of foreign origin but, just like kebab, completely integrated in local foodways.

Both kebab and couscous have become mainstays in many European countries. A book was recently published in Poland with the title *Kebabistan: About the Polish National Dish*.[2] While the author's intention was obviously provocative, the data he provides point to kebab's success in the Central Eastern European country. In 2016 it was the first eating-out choice for 45 percent of people. The following year, although falling to 40 percent, it became the most popular, right before pizza (another food with a foreign origin) and "Polish food." Even participants in the right-wing xenophobic demonstrations that in recent years have taken place in Polish cities happily patronize kebab places right after the rallies, though some of those same eateries may have been damaged during the events. This state of affairs baffles conservatives who extoll the virtues of traditional dishes as an expression of proper Polishness, family values, and Christian culture and those who, embracing non-exclusionary gastronativist positions, are "rediscovering" and "elevating" Polish cuisine according to the standards of cosmopolitan gourmets.

In fact, in Europe kebab has mostly become the domain of Turkish immigrants in Germany, who have set up efficient manufacture plants where the cylinders of meat are assembled and frozen to be shipped all over the continent, leveraging the network of Turkish traders who are often connected with other Middle Eastern and North African immigrant food entrepreneurs despite the differences in culture and language.[3] The vast majority of consumers are not aware that they are eating a frozen product imported from Germany. Of course, restaurants that make kebab from scratch do exist, but their inevitably higher costs make them favorites of gourmets and those who are willing and able to pay more to enjoy what they perceive as authenticity.

Migrants' ingredients and dishes can generate ambivalence also when the newcomers are not foreign but arrive from less developed areas of the same country. The food of Southern Italians who moved to the northern regions of the country in the 1960s was at first suspicious, only to become a beloved addition to the local food scene over time.[4] Specialties introduced since the 1910s by African Americans moving from the rural South of the U.S. to northern cities during the Great Migration were initially derided as uncouth and backward by urban African Americans, only to turn into symbols of pride as "soul food."[5] In large coastal Chinese cities, the meat skewers and spicy lamb noodles cooked by ethnic Uighurs displaced from their places of origin by a massive inflow of ethnic Chinese, are both popular and exotic.[6] Dispossessed farmers from the arid Brazilian Northeast who migrate to large southern cities as cooks or service staff often see their food publicly scorned but privately appreciated by the families for whom they work.[7] The examples are countless.

IMMIGRATION AND GASTRONATIVISM

Attitudes toward migrants are shaped not only by high-profile political debates but also through everyday interactions among neighbors, fellow commuters, and—let's not forget it—participants in the food system. When it comes to what we eat, where food comes from, who prepares it for us, and who sits at our table, all bets are off. What we eat becomes us. Nothing is more straightforward, intimate, and visceral. Fear of the unknown is inevitable, while the exploration of new possibilities promises excitement. As a consequence, the food of immigrants, redolent of peculiar aromas and bursting with unfamiliar flavors, easily get entangled in polemics that go well beyond the gustatory and touch on the political. It excites attraction and revulsion, interest and rejection.

Not surprisingly, the food cultures of immigrants are among the bogeymen that exclusionary gastronativism most frequently exploits. Their ingredients, their dishes, and their practices are vilified as coarse, lacking in nutrition, or outright disgusting. Such refusal becomes one with the condemnation of supposedly globalist, cosmopolitan, and elitist attitudes that instead highlight the contribution of migrant cuisines to a country's multiculturality and sense of modernity. However, also in that case, the acceptance and popularity of ethnic or migrant culinary traditions are not necessarily indicative of the cultural and social integration of the communities behind them.

The growing presence of domestic and foreign migrants in the most developed areas of mid-income and high-income countries is the result of the mass displacement that has intensified in recent decades as a consequence of the neoliberal model of globalization, worsening effects of climate change, and high rates of urbanization, with 55 percent of the world population living in cities as of 2019.[8] These factors also contribute to local and regional political instabilities that frequently explode into armed conflicts, further intensifying migratory movements. Inevitably, due to their sheer numbers, migrants have turned into flashpoints for gastronativist controversies, political debates, and, unfortunately, violence. The presence of outsiders may trouble or enrage blue-collar workers watching their jobs disappear and their acquired privileges being stripped away. Their worries can be amplified by run-of-the-mill, more or less overt racists bent on defending their biological purity, their assumed cultural superiority, and their way of life. As food does not require much explanation and is accessible to everybody, expressions of exclusionary gastronativism can be easily fomented, manipulated, or exploited by politicians and chauvinistic movements.

Migrants are more frequently sympathized with as victims in the nonexclusionary gastronativism we observed in food movements, especially when their adherents share liberal views and their jobs and quality of life are not threatened by the newcomers. To those who resent and oppose the standardization imposed by transnational corporations, the presence of ethnic restaurants and availability of foreign products makes their cities more interesting and appealing, more cosmopolitan and exciting. Familiarity with immigrants' dishes and their practices is treated as a mark of distinction and cultural capital. Being able to order from an ethnic food truck or navigate a menu in a foreign restaurant is cool. However, these attitudes embody the very essence of the globalism that exclusionary gastronativism decries, especially when practiced by urban, educated elites.

Liberal food movements overall lament the exploitation of immigrants, in particular the undocumented ones, in large agribusinesses, animal farming, and slaughterhouses. Nevertheless, contradictions abound when gourmets' leisure habits have to square with the social concerns of the food movement. While enjoying fresh produce at the farmers market, well-meaning foodies may prefer to stick to the pastoral fantasy of the family farm, overlooking the role immigrant workers play in growing their favorite heirloom tomatoes or tending to the goats that produce milk for their cheese. Foodies may support ethnic entrepreneurs, especially of the mom-and-pop kind, while ignoring the underpaid migrant workers who prep, cook, and dispose of food in nonethnic restaurants, deliver their meals, and stock the shelves of their grocery stores. They may be all for urban farming, blissfully unaware of the racial and ethnic inequalities that determine who has access to space and inputs.[9]

Those that embrace more political and activist attitudes as members of antiglobalization movements envision a multicultural society where immigrants have their place, as they are potential allies in the fight against global elites and transnational centers of economic and political power. Some organizations, like the European No Border network, favor free international migration and the elimination of border controls. Paradoxically, the absence of frontiers may also be advantageous for the movers and shakers of neoliberal globalization. Although it is politically risky to admit it, many employers in the agriculture, food-processing, and food service sectors of high-income countries are not totally against a less controlled presence of low-skilled migrant workers, as they constitute a cheap labor pool. When they are undocumented, migrants are even more susceptible to exploitation, regardless of labor regulations and basic human rights.

The nonexclusionary gastronativism of rural and peasant movements usually express solidarity toward migrants, who are considered victims of the same globalizing forces that threaten the food sovereignty of their own communities. As La Via Campesina asserted in its 2015 Declaration on Migration and Rural Workers, "aggressive policies that impose a development model based on the exploitation of resources, the grabbing of the commons, the stealing of agricultural lands and the exploitation of peasants as well as that of women and men who work the land, have a particularly harsh effect on peasant communities. Ruined people have no other option [but] to leave family, land and community to seek the means of survival someplace else, in the big cities or in any countries."[10] As relatively few migrants settle down in the countryside, especially avoiding already downtrodden areas where jobs are hard to come by, thus far limited tensions seem to have emerged between rural food sovereignty movements and migrants.

CULINARY COMPETENCE

Food is especially relevant in the debates around the presence of migrants because it is one of the most important aspects of everyday life newcomers turn to when coping with the dislocation and disorientation they experience in new and unknown spaces. They recreate a sense of place around what they cook and consume together. These factors make food a particularly visible aspect of migrant communities, which are often identified and stereotyped based on their eating habits and their preferences. Time and again, food becomes one of the first point of encounter or clash with the host communities. However, regardless of ideological declarations or political positions, processes of acculturation, hybridization, fusion, and, at times, appropriation of migrants' food are extremely frequent. Despite the tendency to essentialize ethnic food as something distinct from local, traditional, and national foodways, the reality is quite different.

Since migrants are active agents in these processes, it is important to examine how they experience their own food in new places, how they adapt to shifting situations and contexts, and how they turn their culinary traditions into opportunities for entrepreneurship or, simply, for acceptance. Of course, migrants do not have access to the same resources and power as members of their host communities. The street vendor of tortillas, as successful as she may be, does not have the same opportunities for determining what, how, and to whom she sells; she may be open to changing her recipes to please local customers; she may have to negotiate constantly with the police, health authorities, and local government officers. We should refrain from romanticizing culinary integration: adaptation and assimilation can be painful.[11]

Migrants' food cultures are influenced not only by their past but also by their current situations. As a result, meanings migrants attribute to their own food are never completely defined once and for all but are endlessly negotiated and transformed in everyday life.¹² Certain food objects, behaviors, and norms from their places of origin are maintained, more or less transformed, to become important points of reference in the formation of a new sense of community and identity. Some may instead disappear, while others resurface only after periods of invisibility. Unfamiliar elements from host communities can be absorbed, ignored, or despised. However, despite these constant transformations, migrants' food cultures present an internal coherence, which provides parameters that define behaviors and objects as acceptable or deviant. Such implicit rules can be interpreted as a form of "culinary competence" acquired through food production, preparation, and consumption.

Such competence functions as a compass for immigrants who find themselves negotiating their sense of culinary identity in new places. They bring with them specific "techniques of the body," which anthropologist Marcel Mauss described as "the ways in which from society to society men [in the sense of humans] know how to use their bodies."¹³ These techniques, which include correct behaviors during meals, the control of bodily functions, and the gestures related to cooking and eating, are not innate. Children need to learn them slowly and sometimes painfully by imitating adults and by being explicitly taught. However, customary body techniques can look out of place when practiced in new places: West African or Indian immigrants, for instance, are aware that their preference for eating with their hands is frowned upon in certain areas of the world. Foreigners marvel at the ability of small Italian children to proficiently use forks when eating spaghetti. Only relatively recently has eating with chopsticks become less of an extraordinary skill in Western countries.

Culinary competence operates in four conceptually distinct but often overlapping dimensions: the personal, communal, collective, and institutional spheres of migrants' social life. The personal dimension is the most immediate and idiosyncratic. Individuals find themselves at the juncture of necessity, external inputs, and their inner world of feelings, memories, desires, and instincts.[14] Eating forces them to interact physically, emotionally, and cognitively with the new environment. Reactions may vary enormously in terms of involvement with foreign culinary practices, ranging from enthusiastic embrace and participative negotiation to active resistance—all the way to total refusal. Like anybody else, migrants experience the tension between neophilia and neophobia we explored in chapter 3. Through these interactions inside and outside their familiar circles, they transform anonymous and threatening spaces into significant and culturally meaningful places that blur the apparent opposition between the global and the local.

The personal understanding and utilization of food is enriched by the contributions of others who share the same background, establishing a "communal" dimension. Unless migrants are alone and refrain from any contact, the adaptation process to the new situation is shared, influenced, and constructed through interactions with the intimate circles of family, friends, neighbors, and coworkers. These connections are particularly important as migrants must adjust to puzzling seasonal cycles, foreign calendars, and strange holidays where their food plays no part. When they long for their traditional recipes, they may rely on those closer to them to get the right ingredients and tools or to learn how to prepare them.

If they do not find the exact products they were used to, they may be compelled to make substitutions with other products as similar as possible to the original ones. They slowly adjust to their new settings, expanding and changing their culinary competence while negotiating with those around them. Beginning in the early twentieth century, Italian immigrants in the Americas, from Canada to Argentina, slowly integrated more meat in their everyday dishes because it was more available and affordable in the New World. Reacting to the newfound abundance, portions became larger, and festive dishes became everyday fare.[15] The adaptation did not get to the point of renouncing certain food such as anchovies or olive oil, which continued to be imported from Italy.[16] For Indian immigrants, wherever they settled, some of the spices that compose their complex palettes of masalas could not be easily substituted: the choice was between renouncing or importing them. Trade networks were slowly set up to secure access to spices and other relevant ingredients.[17] The larger the migrant community, the more profitable was such commerce.

As migrants expand and reshape their culinary competence to adapt to their changed conditions, the communal repository of memories and experiences from their place of origin may also influence the way they relate to each other. While easing the anxieties caused by the constant and invasive exposure to the new environment, communal practices such as food preparation, shopping, and celebratory meals strengthen a sense of belonging. However, these can become sources of emotional ambivalence between the need for comfort foods that echoes the immigrants' past and the awareness that the consumption of those very foods might mark them as outsiders in the host society in terms of flavors, smells, and materials. As important for the cultural reproduction of social life as they may be, such foods and practices frequently undergo negotiations in which not all members of migrant communities enjoy the same level of power or privilege.

MIGRANT FOOD AS BUSINESS

Food also allows migrants to establish food production and distribution activities that provide vital sources of employment and contribute to shaping their public identity. Nationalism, political ideologies, as well as religious, cultural, and ethnic components merge with economic priorities to construct diasporic identities.[18] Through stores, restaurants, and food manufacturing, immigrants develop tactics that employ their culinary know-how to improve their social and economic position by transforming not only their fellow newcomers but also the members of the host community into customers and consumers of their products.[19] In so doing, they become parts of networks that span from their block to their workplace, the importing companies from which they buy the necessary ingredients, and the kitchens where more or less traditional or innovative interpretations of familiar dishes are prepared. Migrant entrepreneurs can experience their community as a network of food producers, distributors, consumers, physical spaces such as malls, supermarkets, and markets, as well as means of transportation, phones, and the Internet, the banking system, cash money, and mailing lists. The marketplace often contributes to maintaining connections with their places of origin and their culinary cultures as well as with other communities in the diaspora. However, participation in the food business does not automatically imply agency and autonomy: migrants are easily exploited and forced into menial occupations with no space for creativity or advancement.

Restaurants loom large in immigrant narratives. In them, negotiations take place between waves of migrants and patrons from various backgrounds with different preferences and spending capacity. The result can be the emergence of cuisines with standardized menus and dishes that, over time, became familiar both to restaurant goers from the host community and the immigrant communities themselves, especially when they come from regions of the same country with different culinary cultures. Regional peculiarities get blurred, only to reappear and acquire value when the ethnic cuisine becomes the object of interest of foodies and culinary experts. Chinese restaurants now distinguish themselves by offering Sichuan, Henan, or Shanghai specialties, often vying for a clientele that is always looking for something new and exciting. Food connoisseurs who discretely yawn when presented with Tuscan or Neapolitan food may get more excited about the less-known culinary traditions of Italian regions like Sardinia or Abruzzo.

In the contemporary metropolis, immigrant-owned restaurants have to measure themselves with those serving food from other migrant communities. As food scholar Krishnendu Ray explains, however, not all ethnic cuisines are equal: for instance, in the U.S., Italian and Japanese currently enjoy higher status than Mexican or Chinese, a stratification directly reflected in the prices restaurants can command.[20] The reasons for these differences may lie in the extent to which each community has been absorbed into the mainstream, their success and visibility in other social spheres, or their connections with prestigious countries of origin.

Migrants' personal and communal experiences are often embedded in and influenced by practices, norms, and representations that could be defined as "collective." The collective dimension transcends individuals and tightly knit social groups that presuppose personal acquaintance among members. Collective experiences are supposed to be shared by individuals and groups that might not be in direct contact but somehow share the same origin and story, considering themselves as part of the same diasporic community, spread out as it may be around the world. For example, groups of immigrants coming from different parts of China to the U.S. at different points in time with different motivations, speaking mutually unintelligible languages and eating very distinctive food, found themselves establishing a new shared identity as Chinese. The host community bunched them into an undifferentiated group, and they often lived in the same neighborhoods, had similar jobs, and interacted in a variety of social activities. Recipes started circulating beyond immediate circles of acquaintances, importers provided certain products and not others, and a set of holidays and relevant occasions slowly acquired more importance than others.[21] As transportation and communication technologies improve, the contacts between diasporic groups from the same place of origin increase and intensify their exchanges and contacts, wherever they are located in the world. Young Chinese migrants are fully aware of what happens to their compatriots, regardless of their location. Social media has only made these kinds of connections easier and more immediate.

The "collective" aspect of migrant culinary experiences is constructed through constant interactions not only among members of a diaspora and their host communities but also with their communities of provenance. Many migrants, especially in the first generation, frequently maintain close ties with their place of origin through relatives, friends, remittances, participation in events and special occasions, and occasional trips. However, immigrant culinary canons often develop following their own dynamics, not necessarily the same, that shape their cuisine of origin in the same period of time: the context, the external pressures, and the internal structures are not the same. Within these canons, dishes and practices linked to special occasions and celebrations assume particular visibility and relevance. We can mention the Italian American Seven Fish dinner on Christmas Eve, the Seder dinner for Passover in Jewish communities, Lunar New Year dishes for immigrants of Chinese descent, Diwali specialties for Hindus, sweets for the Mexican Día de Muertos, and street food sold at the annual Caribbean parade in Brooklyn. Interestingly, these practices have the potential to become objects of dissension among older and younger generations who might have very different takes on their relevance in the new environment. Furthermore, food-related traditions are filtered through cookbooks, media, and other discursive elements that, over time, establish conventions and expectations, often shared and reinforced by the host community.

The last aspect of migrant experiences can be defined as "institutional," referring to practices and representations shaped and sustained by public and private institutions as diverse as business firms, cultural institutes, and governments. Such dimension is explicitly meant to immortalize, protect, and promote specific foods and food practices. Some of the activities that reflect this dimension have been discussed in the previous two chapters, as they fall in the domain of diplomacy and trade. For instance, what is the impact on Italian pizza makers around the world of the inscription of the "Art of the Neapolitan pizzaiuolo" in the UNESCO list of Intangible Cultural Heritage? How does the inclusion in the list of the Turkish coffee culture and tradition influence the practices of Turkish cafe owners outside of Turkey? What about the expectations of their clients? To circle back to couscous, will the successful addition to the UNESCO list of "the knowledge, know-how and practices related to the production and consumption of couscous," following the initiatives of four Maghreb governments, change its perception and appreciation in France?

Migrant foods are never isolated. They are never totally "other." To the dismay of those who would like to keep a distance from them, they are dynamically involved in shifting networks that include not only immigrants but also the very host communities that variously despise them, ignore them, or embrace them as enrichment. For this reason, exclusionary gastronativism frequently turn migrants and their foodways into targets for their discourses and their political strategies, depicting them as threats that can penetrate the body politics in deceptive and secretive ways to destroy it from within. Just like a virus . . .

Chapter Nine

CONTAGIONS

WAS IT eating bats or pangolins that started the COVID-19 pandemic? By early 2020, despite denials from the Chinese authorities, the first cases of the new coronavirus were attributed to contact with wild animals sold at the Huanan Seafood Wholesale Market in Wuhan, China, where it was suspected that dubious sanitary conditions had allowed the virus to leap to humans. Such occurrences are not uncommon in societies in which certain wild animals are coveted because of the cultural and medicinal value attributed to their consumption and their hunting and sale are widely practiced as a supplementary source of revenue to make up for lack of employment or low wages. In the rest of the world, fear of the contagion was amplified by the identification of its causes with forms of food consumption that are considered disgusting and barbaric. Nevertheless, in the spring of 2021, suspicions that the virus was man-made and escaped from a laboratory in Wuhan led to requests for further investigation, amidst international bruhaha. In reality, it is extremely difficult to determine the exact origin of a pandemic. For example, it is still unclear whether the so-called Spanish influenza that killed over forty million people between 1918 and 1920 started in the United States, in the Austro-Hungarian Empire, or in China.[1]

It is easy to place the blame for pandemics onto others, externalizing the sense of danger and focusing it on exotic food traditions and customs. However, we should not forget that the advanced and supposedly safe zootechnics practiced in the Global North can breed viruses and antibiotic-resistant bacteria.[2] The debates on the source of the virus have moved well beyond scientific inquiries to gain traction as ideological tools of considerable impact. The geopolitical implications are evident. In the U.S., where China is widely perceived as a political, economic, and cultural threat, former president Donald Trump referred to COVID-19 as the "Chinese virus," "kung flu," a "foreign virus," and a treacherous "invisible enemy." After some hesitancy, his successor president Joe Biden also called for greater access to China's labs to conduct a more thorough investigation.

All parties concerned played the blame game. In June 2020, when China had apparently managed to control the virus, a new outbreak was identified around the Xinfadi Market in Beijing, where fish, fruit, and vegetables (not exotic animals) are sold wholesale. Initially, news spread that the virus had been found on a cutting board used for imported salmon. The resurgence of the pandemic was immediately attributed to foreign actors, increasing the climate of mistrust and nationalism in the country. Despite the rumors about salmon resulting to be false, Chinese consumers stopped buying it, with enormous economic damage to exporting countries such as Norway and Chile.[3] They also began avoiding seafood restaurants, with significant repercussions on the hospitality sector, which was just recovering from the first draconian lockdown. Imports of poultry from the Tyson company, one of the largest in the U.S., were also suspended because of large numbers of infected workers at its plants.[4] COVID-19 has put the circulation of commodities across borders to the test, making the weaknesses in the global food system glaringly obvious.

THE POWER OF METAPHORS

Hygiene is the immediate and efficient response to the dangers hidden in what we eat. Science and technology become weapons of defense and control against invasive foreign intruders, especially invisible ones. When, as in the case of COVID-19, the virus is new and the scientific community is struggling to understand it while trying to limit its impact, panic is inevitable. Plenty of questions did not have immediate answers: How does it spread? Does it survive on food and packaging? Is it resistant to sun and heat? How can we protect ourselves when we go shopping? Can we eat out at restaurants? What about a morning coffee at a café?

Alarm provided fertile terrain for gastronativist arguments to develop. Metaphors of pathogens and infection, vaccination and defense are particularly powerful. Metaphors, often based on our body and how it exists and moves in the world, help us make sense of abstract issues. They affect assumptions of which we may not be fully aware and the vocabulary we rely on to frame and understand reality. To some extent, they influence not only how we think about our surroundings but also how we operate in it.[5] Both neuroscience and philosophy suggest that metaphors contribute to shaping our everyday decisions.[6] As they can be applied to different aspects of social life, metaphors can solidify harmful worldviews and stereotypes, often naturalizing them and making them invisible. The metaphor of contagion has been reinforced and amplified by global experiences of quarantine and social distancing, which have profoundly modified interactions among individuals, families, communities, and nations.

Based on trustworthy foundations provided by medicine and scientific research, common knowledge about pathogens provides tools, however limited and imperfect, to make sense of phenomena of enormous significance, somewhat easing anxieties about contagion. The virus becomes a metaphor for all external dangers that subtly penetrate the body politic and for all political corruption that spreads uncontrollably and attacks the foundations of civilized life from inside.[7] Autocrats, politicians, and movement leaders have effortlessly exploited the metaphor of the virus to drive home ideological points while shrouding them in science and common sense. In the case of COVID-19, the metaphor is ever more effective because it is also connected to food, which penetrates the depths of the body and, as such, is the object of intense concerns, emerging as a strategic tool in gastronativist strategies, as we saw in chapter 3.

The metaphor of contagion is used to frame not only international relations but also domestic tensions within individual countries, where elements outside the mainstream can be represented as devious agents of moral corruption. The poor, members of ethnic minorities, and migrants frequently end up being described not only as intrusive destabilizers of society but also as dirty carriers of medical diseases. For example, in 2015, then presidential candidate Donald Trump declared, "Tremendous infectious disease is pouring across the border," while denouncing the growing numbers of undocumented immigrants in the U.S.[8] In the same year, when he was still the leader of the opposition, the current strongman of conservative politics in Poland, Jarosław Kaczyński, famously declared that migrants bring "all sorts of parasites and protozoa."[9] The following year, Hungarian leader Viktor Orban compared asylum seekers to "poison."[10]

Such sentiments were amplified during the COVID-19 pandemic. Migrants were at times portrayed as a force determined to shrewdly take advantage of the generosity of host countries while destroying their institutions, culture, and social fabric. In this worldview, often imbued with racism, the body politic is constantly exposed to risk if adequate protection measures are not taken, ranging from regulations barring newcomers to the physical construction of fences and walls. Moral panic caused by urbanization, secularization, and demographic shifts can find scapegoats in migrants, diverting attention from domestic structural issues of injustice and exploitation. It does not take much to extend the metaphor of infectious migrants to their food, intensifying the gastronativist approaches we explored in the previous chapter.

FOOD DESTROYERS

Metaphors built around the idea of contagion, which often carry strong connotations of invasion, siege, and defense, also apply to plant or animal species that are not native to a specific location but, accidentally or deliberately introduced by man, have multiplied to the point of devastating entire ecological systems, often severely damaging food production. Due to their capacity to grow and reproduce rapidly, these invasive species are figuratively attributed free will and self-determination, just like unwanted immigrants.[11] Kudzu (*Pueraria lobata*) became popular in the U.S. in the second half of the nineteenth century as an ornamental climbing plant and was touted by the Soil Conservation Service (now Natural Resources Conservation Service) in the years before World War II as a tool to limit erosion on agricultural land in the southeast of the country.[12] Only later was the plant classified as an invasive species capable of enormous ecological damage. Today great efforts and expense are dedicated to its destruction. The Asian carp was introduced into fish farming ponds in the southern U.S. in the 1970s and spread rapidly up the Mississippi.[13] The fish has decimated several native species, and various methods are currently being investigated to prevent it from colonizing the Great Lakes. Although invasive species are often perfectly edible, their consumption is limited by their perception as polluting and unsafe.

Sometimes the threat is less visible, as in the case of the *Xylella fastidiosa* bacterium, which until the first decade of the twenty-first century was mainly limited to the Americas. It later spread to France and more recently to Puglia, in southern

Italy, where it affected olive trees.[14] In the mid-nineteenth century, the potato blight caused the loss of whole tuber crops in Ireland, triggering the political and economic downward spiral that led to a tragic famine. In the second half of the nineteenth century, the insect pest *phylloxera* almost completely wiped out European wine production.[15] The Panama disease, caused by the pathogenic fungus *Fusarium oxysporum*, devastated the Gros Michel banana variety in the 1950s, the most common at the time. The disaster forced producers to introduce the Cavendish variety, which is now the most planted internationally but is itself threatened by new strains of the same disease. In fact, the infection has already spread to crops in South and Southeast Asia, spurring feverish research for more resistant varieties. Similarly, coffee production is besieged by *Hemileia vastatrix*, a fungus also known as coffee rust, which, although little known to the general public, is causing anxiety for the entire industry. Danger in the form of invisible but deadly invaders is always lurking, threatening to decimate our food production.

Pathogens and diseases also affect animal husbandry, breeding panic among citizens and creating international commercial and political tensions. In November 1986, the first official case of mad cow disease, or bovine spongiform encephalopathy (BSE), was detected in British cattle. The cause of the epidemic was identified with prions that multiplied in the carcasses and offal of animals, particularly sheep, which were then processed into dietary supplements for livestock without steam sterilization at high temperatures. Although the pathogens could be transmitted to humans who ate beef, causing the lethal Creutzfeldt-Jakob disease, attempts were made to hide outbreaks to protect the UK beef sector. In 1989, the European Union imposed an embargo on British exports of veal over six months of age, and in 1994 it banned the use of dietary supplements for livestock derived from other animals. In 1996, the Union voted in favor of a total ban on imports of beef from the UK, whereby the British government decided to kill cows over thirty months of age and destroy their carcasses.[16]

The avian flu that spread between 2003 and 2006 showed how fear of invisible invaders in the food system can impact society at large. In Italy, for example, Asian food and restaurants were stigmatized, as consumers feared that goods from Asia were contaminated, while poultry consumption decreased.[17] Those worries amplified the widespread belief that the Chinese entrepreneurs used low-quality or expired frozen foods imported from their homeland, which explained the low prices they charged. The concerns were confirmed by actual criminal cases, which, however, were extremely limited in number. Consumers ignored the most important factor behind the low cost, namely the employment of family members and newly arrived immigrants.[18] At the time, several Chinese restaurants had to become pizzerias to ensure their survival. Unfortunately, similar phenomena reappeared during the COVID-19 pandemic in Italy and elsewhere as an expression of gastronativist instincts overlapping with often virulent anti-Asian prejudice.[19]

INVADERS ALL AROUND

The anxieties related to foreign bodies and the metaphors they generate appear not only in issues concerning food, migrants, and ethnic or cultural minorities but also in other areas of social life, such as information technology and communication, revealing their strong cultural relevance in the contemporary world. We are now haunted by the alarm caused by hackers and digital viruses that can infect hard drives, operating systems, and cyber clouds, wreaking havoc on entire networks. Suffice it to recall the Y2K panic, caused by the fear of possible damage to the functioning of computers that swept the world on the threshold of the new millennium. We are all worried about the possibility, unfortunately very real, that apparently harmless messages or pictures from friends and family may contain malicious software that could make our computers and smartphones unusable, spreading to all those with whom we are in virtual contact. Criminal organizations, at times backed by national governments, have the capabilities to install software in computer systems that can spy and steal information or paralyze entire organizations: like parasites, they penetrate furtively, steal precious elements, or lead to destruction. However, it is interesting that these dynamics, based on bits and bytes, electronic memories and digital functions, are also conceptualized in terms of viruses and infections, expressing broader anxieties about unpredictable and destructive contagions.

The same concerns, similarly connected with aspects of our daily life that relate to technology, are expressed in the field of communication to describe the spread of fake news on social media, a favorite tool in exclusionary gastronativism. Any piece of information can now be approached as a falsehood propagated with the aim of influencing the public opinion. Such worries are based on reality: there are companies specialized in the manufacture and diffusion of fake news that are all the more dangerous the more they seem harmless. Just like infections. Also, in cases where there is no criminal intent, when a piece of news, a video, or a meme is exchanged with very high frequency among social media users, we say it goes "viral."

The effectiveness of metaphors related to parasites, viruses, and infection therefore appears to be connected to fears regarding aspects of our life that for various reasons remain difficult to understand and require specific knowledge. Few have the necessary level of education and training, and in any case many distrust expertise as an expression of an elitist culture that disregards the opinions and the ideas of ordinary persons, while using big words and complicated concepts to hide power grabs.

Furthermore, the past few years have seen the diffusion of conspiracy mindsets that are fixated on dark plots and evil schemes, allegedly organized by small groups of corrupt and powerful people (generally identified with traditional economic, political, or cultural elites) whose identities remain secret. In this worldview, extraordinary events such as pandemics, recessions, or terrorist attacks take place at the behest of secret cabals committed to controlling society and directing the destinies of the world for their sole advantage.[20]

It would seem that the risk society, evoked by Ulrich Beck as a result of the lack of control and certainties in our fast-shifting reality, both expresses its deepest fears and finds them constantly confirmed through metaphors of contagion, infection, and other subtle forms of intrusion.[21] Against this background, looking at how gastronativism employs these metaphors in the realm of food can provide a unique lens to explore other social phenomena that, apparently unrelated, reveal common roots and can be similarly exploited for political goals.

HUMANS AND MICROORGANISMS

The relationship between the body (both individual and collective) and the enemies that attack it, especially when the contagion operates through food, is so emotionally and culturally powerful that it distorts the perception of scientific facts. Not only viruses and bacteria but also hormones, pesticides, fertilizers, and other types of invisible contaminants can elicit intense reactions, particularly among those who hold nonexclusionary gastronativist positions, from the food movement to antiglobalization activists. Viruses are often conceptualized as invasive species and active living beings, whereas in reality they are subcellular bundles of genetic code that are not even capable of self-replicating: it is the infected cells that multiply them with devastating effect.[22] Nevertheless, infectious microorganisms are often anthropomorphized as agents endowed with their own will, bent on taking advantage of their hosts to the point of exhausting their vital force. Their goals are the penetration and defeat of human beings. Such threats require action, providing a perfect breeding ground for ideological instrumentalization.

However, the relationship between humans and microorganisms is at least ambivalent. It is undeniable that bacteria and viruses related to food can be dangerous or deadly (just think of salmonella or E.coli) and that certain molds damage food or can be toxic. Other molds, nevertheless, are responsible for refined drinks and foods: Sauternes wine develops its unique aromas thanks to the presence of *Botrytis cinerea* on the grapes, and the Mexican delicacy *huitlacoche* is the growth of the fungus *Ustilago maydis* on corn. *Penicillium roqueforti* generates the characteristic blue-green veins of Roquefort cheese. Cheese and yogurt are the result of the action of bacteria, and for this reason several countries have taken fairly rigid positions on raw milk products, regardless of their undeniable organoleptic qualities. Fermentation processes are central to the preparation of specialties ranging from Korean kimchi to kombucha and the Polish fermented vegetables *kiszonki*. Not to mention the action of bread yeasts . . . During the COVID-19 pandemic, flocks of home bakers became experts in sourdoughs, lovingly cared for and exchanged among enthusiasts. When it comes to food, not all microorganisms can be considered dangerous invaders. Sometimes they are allies and collaborators.

Whether we appreciate it or not, cohabitation between humans and microorganisms of all kinds is inevitable. Even the most superficial reflection on the relationship between food and the body makes any illusion of self-containment laughable. Our digestive system is open to the environment. Through food, we are deeply connected to and often dependent on weather, soil, plants, animals, and other humans with whom we endlessly swap bacteria and microorganisms. Bodies are porous and integrated into complex ecologies. New studies indicate that intricate mycorrhizal networks made of interwoven hyphae (the microfilaments connecting plant systems and various fungi) function as tools for communication and transport of nutrients among individuals of different plant species scattered over vast areas. Fungi hyphae give minerals to trees, receiving sugars in return and creating communities we have only recently begun to understand.[23]

Our body is anything but self-sufficient. Wendy Garret, an immunologist at Harvard, explains: "We're used to thinking about microbes as enemies—as major threats to our health—but most microbes don't cause disease. They actually help us live better... We are symbionts: human cells coexisting with bacterial cells, fungi, viruses, and parasites. We're multispecies beings."[24] Obviously, these perspectives are to be harmonized with the need for vaccines against pathogens that we know to be harmful. Few microbiologists would align themselves with antivax positions, which paradoxically have flourished as a consequence of COVID-19.

Research on the human microbiota, that is, the "ecological community of commensal, symbiotic, and pathogenic microorganisms" that share our body and are now indicated as both a possible cause and a solution to many diseases, is developing rapidly.[25] Science journalist Ed Yong states:

> We exist in symbiosis—a wonderful term that refers to different organisms living together. Some animals are colonised by microbes while they are still unfertilised eggs; others pick up their first partners at the moment of birth. We then proceed through our lives in their presence.... When we eat, so do they. When we travel, they come along. When we die, they consume us. Every one of us is a zoo in our own right—a colony enclosed within a single body. A multi-species collective. An entire world.... A single animal is full of

ecosystems too. Skin, mouth, guts, genitals, any organ that connects with the outside world: each has its own characteristic community of microbes.[26]

The concept of an ecosystem is central to this line of research. Journalist Michael Specter wrote in the *New Yorker*: "Each of us seems more like a farm than like an individual assembled from a rulebook of genetic instructions. Medicine becomes a matter of cultivation, as if our bacterial cells were crops in a field."[27] The metaphor connects our body functions with food production, proposing a model based on collaboration with what is different from us to achieve not only survival but also good health. If we rethink the meaning of individuality and independence, we could start considering microorganisms as coproducers of human well-being instead of exclusively destroyers.

Problems arise when the balance of the microbiota ecosystem is disturbed by the excessive multiplication of specific bacteria or the improper use of antibiotics. New research focuses on the relationships between gut microbiota, metabolism, absorption, and weight gain.[28] The goal is, in the future, to be able to intervene on these mechanisms through the consumption of live probiotic bacteria,[29] the ingestion of nutrients that can facilitate the growth of specific components of the microbiota, and fecal transplant, i.e., the transfer of macrobiota of healthy individuals to the gastrointestinal tract of subjects suffering from diseases ranging from allergies to autoimmune diseases.[30]

Could these scientific advances also have an impact on metaphors of contagion and how they are exploited in gastronativism? French philosopher Michel Serres pointed out that the word *parasite* literally means something that eats next to something else. The word can refer not only to an entity that consumes food and drink without returning anything but also to those who eat nearby and to symbiotic partners who live in a constant and productive exchange with their guests.[31] The parasite can be understood according to the logic of duality and opposition, easily used as a metaphor in political projects aimed at the exclusion or even the elimination of what is foreign. Migrants are often described both as infections that threaten local cultures and customs and as profiteers of the services that citizens pay for with taxes, without considering that entrepreneurs and migrant workers, if they are regular residents, pay taxes as well. Other groups that do not conform with what is perceived as mainstream, no matter whether their difference is based on gender, age, geographical provenance, class, or ethnic and racial identities, constantly risk being treated as domestic threats bent on corroding the community from inside. But what if we actually need parasites to thrive? What if our health depended on contacts and exchanges with what is foreign to us or among distinctive elements coexisting inside us? Could scientific research introduce different models to think about society, leading us to reevaluate not only the role of the "others" but also the way we approach their food? Could different metaphors of contagion emerge from these ideas, weakening the arguments of exclusionary gastronativism and its ideological clout?

CONCLUSION

WHAT FUTURE?

AS NOBEL laureate Elias Canetti poignantly stated in his masterpiece *Crowds and Power*, "Everything which is eaten is the food of power."[1] In a section fittingly called "The Entrails of Power," Canetti argues that teeth are "the very first manifestation of order," "the most striking natural instrument of power."[2] Power asserts itself as a form of digestion that sucks all substance from those it is supposed to represent. It is not by chance that, in the past, kings had to show their authority and prowess by their unusual capacity for ingestion, often resulting in full bodies and visible bellies. These days, power may try to disguise itself in slim and toned bodies that are subjected to all kinds of training to display eternal youth and fitness, but the goals remain the same. Power is fortified by the fear of being destroyed and consumed by stronger enemies.

Nothing is simple about food. The debates and controversies that surround it are rarely just about what and how we eat. For this reason, their study can offer insights to better understand current events. I have proposed gastronativism as a tool to navigate the relationship between food and power that Canetti exposed. Gastronativism can be defined as the ideological use of food in politics to advance ideas about who belongs to a community (in any way it may be defined) and who doesn't, to identify threats, and to propose strategies to fight against them. As Benito Mussolini stated in a 1932 interview, "in every society there is a part of citizens that needs to be hated."[3] Moreover, contemporary forms of gastronativism emerge as a reaction to the devastating dynamics of neoliberal globalization, their impact on everyday life, and the anxieties they instigate about the future.

By leveraging concerns about ingesting potentially toxic material, fears for anything that feels too alien, and disgust for what is experienced as physically or morally polluting or both, exclusionary gastronativism shifts from only considering others as different to reviling them as dangerous and threatening. The other becomes the enemy with whom coexistence is impossible. Such tensions can be easily harnessed ideologically because of their emotional intensity and urgency, which are experienced individually but also shared among members of social groupings. As a matter of fact, new alignments coalesce at times as a response to these anxieties. And when a community is in a state of emergency, limitations of civil liberties become more acceptable, making it more expeditious for authoritarian politicians to take control of institutions and governments through democratic elections (where they exist) or through misleading claims about the protections of order, laws, and constitutions against internal and external attacks. Such politicians disingenuously invoke tolerance while at the same time attacking the basic rules of engagement for pluralism and liberal democracy. They muddle the differences between abstract rights and actual power, substantial and formal equality. In the U.S., for instance, they take advantage of the constitutional tension between the freedom of speech guaranteed by First Amendment and the equal protection under the law introduced by the Fourteenth Amendment. Gastronativism becomes functional to these appeals by operating in a field of social activity, food, that impacts the physical body of the individual and the moral body of the community, regardless of how the latter may be defined. As historian Timothy Snyder observed, "propaganda exploits the power of language to generalize from the particular, and the tendency of people to believe general claims they find consistent with their own personal experiences."[4]

Gastronativist discourses and practices are so widespread throughout the world that they have somehow become normalized and readily available ideological trappings that are easy to activate precisely because of the ubiquitous and immediate nature of food. These characteristics have made the value of the gastronativist tool kit obvious to anybody looking to breed outrage and instigate swift reactions, the bread and butter of the echo-chambered polarization that is currently prevalent in many national and global political debates. Food provides a fertile terrain of resistance against the powers that be, as we saw with the food sovereignty movement. However, it can also turn into an instrument for hegemony, all while being ostensibly used to assert autonomy and negotiate dominance. The tactics of activists may end up being channeled to serve the strategies of those who strive to achieve power. Fueled by contemporary mass communication and social media, intolerance grows. Few attempts are made at reciprocal understanding between opponents, as the political discourse is increasingly split. It does not pay to listen to one's antagonists when the main goal is to fire up the base. Each side in gastronativist debates fights to become the hegemonic force and to extend its cultural and political control over the entire community.

In my opinion, however, not all positions are equivalent. The politics underlying exclusionary gastronativism favor the restriction of the rights of minorities through the unbridled rule of the majority or of a minority claiming to be the true soul of a community. Defense of tradition and local cultures can give way to authoritarian streaks that clash with the protection of liberal democracy, although conservative voices constantly decry progressivism's supposed tendency to limit their spaces of expression, especially on cultural and social issues. Nonexclusionary gastronativism tends, instead, to align itself with political projects that support the expansion of rights to the advantage of discriminated minorities and those excluded from decisional processes. In these approaches, aspirations for self-determination and equality may trump the protection of tradition and local cultures, which are nevertheless appreciated as expression of diversity.

An advantage of gastronativism as an analytic lens is that it reveals how many food-related controversies derive from widespread discontent with the existing political and economic arrangements—both domestically and internationally—and the

CONCLUSION

global food system that they support. Neoliberal globalization has generated a mounting sense of insecurity, caused by growing inequalities between the haves and the have-nots. Epochal shifts in terms of technology, the lack of stable jobs for millennials and Gen Zers, the spread of the gig economy and the demise of unions, job relocations, migrations of displaced populations, and the effects of climate change have wreaked havoc among those who are not equipped to protect themselves from such changes. Instability has made the desire for community and rootedness more urgent, a yearning that takes very different forms in exclusionary and nonexclusionary gastronativist discourses and strategies.

Although the world is obviously not one and the same, gastronativism has emerged as a phenomenon that needs to be examined globally. It may be difficult to shift one's attention from the trees of local and national events to the forests of worldwide horizons. Nevertheless, it is by looking for similarities, shared processes, and common roots that I developed the concept of gastronativism as an attempt to connect and understand events and dynamics in very distant locations. Even so, the goal of this book is not to foresee what is to come but to provide instruments to operate in the reality that surrounds us. We don't know what the future holds in store. There is no destiny, no predetermined conclusion. It is not possible to identify the core engine of history, or even to suppose that one exists: spiritual salvation, class struggle, progress, economic development, and clash of civilizations no longer work as grand explanations for reality. The future is uncertain, and the outcomes depend on innumerable factors.

CONCLUSION

As we discussed, gastronativist activities and attitudes have become more noticeable during the COVID-19 pandemic, as food turned into a pervasive preoccupation for many. Even those who had never thought about it as an issue worthy of attention have shared the troubling feeling that something supposed to be steady and secure is actually not so. Empty shelves, higher prices, and panic hoarding became an alarming reality all over the world. While receiving reassurances about the temporary nature of those disruptions, consumers were shocked by farmers burying their crops back in their fields, meatpacking plants shutting down, and dairy farmers pouring their milk into the sewers just as lines at soup kitchens and food banks were getting longer.

As our daily routines crumbled, we were forced to accept changes in the way we sell, buy, prepare, and consume food, especially in the public sphere. We still don't know what the long-term impact will be on production, distribution, and retail. Will restaurants, catering business, and cafeterias survive? How about military messes or prison canteens? As we are shaken by an apparently unstoppable virus, some of us have looked toward food for comfort; for others, it has become a source of anxiety: in most cases, probably both, allowing for manifestations of gastronativism to appear quite frequently.

As the world is dazed by the far-reaching and still unclear consequences of the pandemic, greater attention has been drawn to the invisible infrastructures, the sophisticated logistics, and the more tangible technological components that allow our food system to function. The crisis has uncovered its structural flaws and inequalities. Food's economic and political relevance will increase for international organizations, national governments, and private companies, especially transnational ones. Their legitimacy will depend on their capacity to ensure enough food at the right time, probably more than before. The growing calls for public interventions, better regulations, collective coordination, and welfare safety nets cannot be simply dismissed. Citizens around the world have realized that, especially in times of crisis, they cannot solve many aspects of the food system by only expressing their preferences through the market.

The events connected with the global pandemic, including the slowing down of foreign trade, concern about migrants as potential spreaders (in contrast to the need for foreign workers), and fear of imported foods as carriers of the disease, have made gastronativist arguments even more compelling. By giving expression to wildly divergent ideas about what society should be like in the future, food turns into an arena for political negotiations between conflicting priorities, needs, and values. The temptation to close ranks and take care of one's own community in times of strain and trauma is strong. Gastronativism could prevail over heterogeneity, receptivity, and integration. Harnessed by exclusionary aspirations, the yearning for well-defined and fixed identities could limit the movement of people, ideas, and materials that has shaped the history of food since the Neolithic.

However, that is not the only possible outcome. At least, we should hope it is not. Food has been instrumental in supporting and providing emotional anchorage to the radicalization of political discontent. We should find ways to turn it into a tool for deradicalization. A deeper awareness of the political,

CONCLUSION

non-neutral quality of all processes defining food traditions and the quest for authenticity can provide a better grasp of the dynamics that allow dishes, products, or customs to be experienced as "local" or "ours." Understanding their emergence and changes over time and space would not diminish their emotional power, but it could blunt their exploitation by belligerent political actors. Appreciation and pride in one's culinary world should not necessarily imply debasing the food of the others. Any community is the result of interactions, clashes, and transformations that point to its very porousness. What we eat today is not what we ate yesterday. And who knows what we will eat tomorrow? By chipping away at ideas of an ageless, essential "us," greater awareness of the possible destructive impulses of gastronativist motivations and strategies could generate more openness toward "them," whoever "they" may be. The answer to the disasters brought about by neoliberal globalization cannot be parochialism or isolation. Our food systems are way too integrated to imagine the total triumph of locavorism. The challenge is to usher modalities of globalization that are more equitable, sustainable, and resilient in case of shocks.

In his work on immigration, published at the turn of the millennium, political scientist Joel Fetzer suggested various possible solutions to nativist excesses, such as education and better media information about immigration's economic and cultural positive impact. He advocated that groups that have suffered persecution in the past should continue teaching the new generations about those events in order to shape their attitudes toward newcomers and the hardships they go through. He also

CONCLUSION

proposed the abolition of the concept of "foreigner," arguing that natives and non-natives should be similar from the point of view of citizenship and access to political rights.[5] After all, I would add, they all pay the same taxes, obey the same laws, and often serve in the same army. Overall, Fetzer looked for answers in the discursive and rational domains. His reflections can be extended to the other minorities, based on gender, sexuality, age, or race and ethnicity, that have been the targets of exclusionary gastronativist actions and proclamations. Twenty years later, considering the growing sway of polarized echo chambers where logic and coherence are secondary, it seems that those strategies, although important, need to be expanded and integrated. The fact I am writing this book proves my faith in intellectual debate, but my experience in public engagement through events and museum exhibitions, my collaborations with designers, and my interactions with the food industry suggest that there are additional dimensions of intervention.

We have discussed the way in which metaphors are central to gastronativist discourses and the practices they underpin. Precisely because food touches on the physical and emotional domains, it may be a good idea to explore countermeasures to exclusionary gastronativism that target the body and feelings. The preparation, sharing, and ingestion of food could offer opportunities to move away from confrontation or, at least, to explore difference. Through such embodied practices, new metaphors could emerge to counteract the ones focusing on threat, invasion, and contagion.

Food as a medium for intercultural communication offers individual and communal experiences that have the potential to

CONCLUSION

elicit strong physical and emotional impressions. Many initiatives already exist that highlight culinary differences not as something to avoid, but rather as an untapped source of pleasure and an immediate entryway to other cultures.[6] Moreover, such initiatives tend to give voice to those who are otherwise kept on the sidelines of society: immigrants, women, the elderly, whose knowledge and expertise turn into assets. Food is also being integrated in school curricula, especially for the lower grades, both as cooking and gardening experiences. Through the appreciation of unfamiliar ingredients, flavors, and textures, young children may be taught to be more open and less fearful toward diversity. However, these attempts may have to counter ingrained conditioning coming from families and their environment, especially in ethnically homogeneous countries.[7] In ethnically diverse countries like the U.S. or the UK, young students are likely to already be exposed to various forms of ethnic foods in their daily lives. In those contexts, the instruction should instead allow immigrant communities to take the lead and present their own culinary traditions on their own terms, beyond the commodified forms students may encounter in restaurants and stores. These experiences could favor interactions that sidestep appropriation, exploitation, and unilateral interpretations by those who hold greater power in terms of cultural mainstream. Such pedagogy could present modes of engagement with material culture that go beyond commodification. The introduction of food as a pedagogical tool is a powerful strategy. If managed properly, it could facilitate real shifts in perceptions and expectation, but effective modalities have to be devised to avoid excessive pushback.

CONCLUSION

These concluding remarks raise questions rather than provide answers. It could not be otherwise, as the food landscape is evolving under our very eyes. It is hard to tell what the post-pandemic world will look like. Not all signs point to positive outcomes: conflicts over vaccines and inequities in their global distribution are far from promising, despite the awareness of new variants of the virus appearing because of low vaccination rates in countries that cannot afford it or are lagging for political reasons. As for the food system, it has not collapsed, as many anticipated or feared. However, it has revealed malfunctions and weak nodes that previously only few were mindful of and, frankly, interested in. Its entanglements with neoliberal globalization have become more evident, uncovering the inequalities and conflicts it produces. These issues are systemic and require the interventions of governments, local authorities, international organizations, NGOs, private companies, civil society, and social movements that can generate structural transformations. Placing food and nutrition at the center of several UN Sustainable Development Goals is not sufficient.

It is up to us all to bring about change through our choices as individuals and our organized actions as citizens. It is up to us to make sure that the events connected with the pandemic will reset the priorities and goals of the global food system, and that the renewed interest in collective initiatives and public interventions will reshape the conditions that have allowed the current ideological uses of food in politics. It is time, at the least, for the most vicious forms of gastronativism to go, once and for all.

NOTES

INTRODUCTION

1. Giorgio Ghiglione, "Pope Francis's Heretical Pasta," *Foreign Policy*, December 24, 2019, https://foreignpolicy.com/2019/12/24/pope-franciss-heretical-pasta/.
2. Fabio Parasecoli, *Al Dente: A History of Food in Italy* (London: Reaktion, 2014).
3. HRW, "India: Vigilante 'Cow Protection' Groups Attack Minorities," *HWR*, February 18, 2019, https://www.hrw.org/report/2019/02/18/violent-cow-protection-india/vigilante-groups-attack-minorities#.
4. Matthias Kamann, "Was setzt die AfD gegen Burkas—Alkohol oder Frauenrechte?, *Welt*, June 7, 2017, https://www.welt.de/politik/deutschland/article165297337/Was-setzt-die-AfD-gegen-Burkas-Alkohol-oder-Frauenrechte.html.
5. Bernhard Forchtner, "The Radical Right and the Meat-Free Diet," *Fair Observer*, June 11, 2018, https://www.fairobserver.com/region/europe/radical-right-neo-nazis-meat-free-diet-vegan-vegetarian-news-51422/.
6. Irina Dumitrescu, "'Bio-Nazis' Go Green in Germany," *Politico*, June 13, 2018, https://www.politico.eu/article/germany-bio-nazis-go-green-natural-farming-right-wing-extremism/.

INTRODUCTION

7. Ma. E., "La polenta uncia contro il cous cous," *La Provincia di Como*, February 7, 2004; F. Angelini, "Straniera la polenta uncia. L'accusa arriva dallo chef," *La Provincia di Como*, February 1, 2010, http://www.laprovinciadicomo.it/stories/Cronaca/214481/.
8. Dondiego, "Et le kebab?" *Mediapart*, September 17, 2017, https://blogs.mediapart.fr/dondiego/blog/170917/et-le-kebab.
9. Francesco Alberti, "E Lucca vieta kebab e cous cous," *Il Corriere*, January 27, 2009, https://www.corriere.it/cronache/09_gennaio_27/lucca_kebab_alberti_7cc435fa-ec4a-11dd-be73-00144f02aabc.shtml.
10. Priscilla Parkhurst-Ferguson, "Culinary Nationalism," *Gastronomica* 10, no. 1: 102–9.
11. Besides the aforementioned work by Priscilla Parkhurst-Ferguson on French culinary nationalism, we can mention Katarzyna Ćwiertka, *Modern Japanese Cuisine: Food, Power, and National Identity* (London: Reaktion, 2007); Michelle T. King, *Culinary Nationalism in Asia* (London: Bloomsbury Academic, 2019); Jeffrey Pilcher, *Que Vivan Los Tamales: Food and the Making of Mexican Identity* (Albuquerque: University of New Mexico Press, 1998); Roberta Sassatelli, ed., *Italians and Food* (Cham: Palgrave Macmillan, 2019); Sandra Sherman, "English Nationalism," *Petits Propos Culinaires* 78 (April 2005): 66–88.
12. Michel Montaigne, *The Complete Essays of Montaigne*, trans. Donald M. Frame (Palo Alto, CA: Stanford University Press, 1965), 152.
13. Michael Hardt and Tony Negri, *Empire* (Cambridge, MA: Harvard University Press, 2000).
14. Philip McMichael, "A Food Regime Genealogy," *Journal of Peasant Studies* 36, no. 1 (2009): 139–69.
15. Michael Lind, *The New Class War: Saving Democracy from the Managerial Elite*, (New York: Portfolio/Penguin, 2020).
16. Thomas Piketty, *Capital in the Twenty-First Century* (Cambridge, MA: Harvard University Press, 2017); Simon Reid-Henry, *The Political Origins of Inequality: Why a More Equal World is Better for Us All* (Chicago: University of Chicago Press, 2015).
17. Ivan Krastev and Stephen Holmes, *The Light That Failed: Why the West Is Losing the Fight for Democracy* (New York: Pegasus, 2019); James Mark, Bogdan Iacob, Tobias Rupprecht, and Ljubica Spaskovska, *1989: A Global History of Eastern Europe* (Cambridge: Cambridge University Press, 2019).
18. Timothy Snyder, "The American Abyss: A Historian of Fascism and Political Atrocity on Trump, the Mob and What Comes Next," *New York*

INTRODUCTION

Times, January 9, 2021, https://www.nytimes.com/2021/01/09/magazine/trump-coup.html.

19. In a 2021 interview, journalist Marsha Gessen pointed out that at their inceptions ideologies are not well thought out, organized worldviews, but they are recognized as such retrospectively, looking at them as history. Throughline, "The Anatomy of Autocracy: Masha Gessen," *NPR*, January 28, 2021, https://www.npr.org/transcripts/960766489.
20. Jason Stanley, *How Fascism Works: The Politics of Us and Them* (New York: Random House, 2018); Timothy Snyder, *On Tyranny: Twenty Lessons from the Twentieth Century* (New York: Tim Duggan, 2017).
21. Benedict Anderson, *Imagined Communities: Reflections on the Origin and Spread of Nationalism* (London: Verso, 1991).
22. Catherine Fischi, *Populocracy: The Tyranny of Authenticity and the Rise of Populism* (Newcastle upon Tyne: Agenda, 2019).
23. Marcel Mauss, *The Gift; Forms and Functions of Exchange in Archaic Societies* (London: Cohen and West, 1966), 76.
24. Ken Albala, ed., *Routledge International Handbook of Food Studies* (Oxon: Routledge, 2013); Warren Belasco, *Food: The Key Concepts* (Oxford: Berg, 2008); Marion Nestle, "Writing the Food Studies Movement," *Food, Culture & Society* 13, no. 2 (2010): 161–70; Willa Zhen, *Food Studies: A Hands-On Guide* (London: Bloomsbury Academic, 2019).
25. Jeff Miller and Jonathan Deutsch, *Food Studies: An Introduction to Research Methods* (Oxford: Berg, 2009), 3.
26. Miller and Deutsch, 4–6.
27. Fabio Parasecoli, *Bite Me: Food in Popular Culture* (Oxford: Berg, 2008); Serena Guidobaldi, *Cibo e identità: l'identità nell'epoca della sua riproducibilità gastronomica* (Torino, Eris, 2021).
28. John Hingham, *Strangers in the Land: Patterns of American Nativism, 1860–1925* (New Brunswick, NJ: Rutgers University Press, 1955), 4.
29. Benjamin R. Knoll and Jordan Shewmaker, "Simply Un-American: Nativism and Support for Health Care Reform," *Political Behavior* 37 (2015): 87–108, 88.
30. Lindsay Peter Huber, Corina Benavides Lopez, Maria C. Malagon, Veronica Velez, and Daniel G. Solorzano, "Getting Beyond the 'Symptom,' Acknowledging the 'Disease': Theorizing Racist Nativism," *Contemporary Justice Review* 11, no. 1 (2008): 39–51, 42.
31. Peter Schrag, *Not Fit for Our Society: Immigration and Nativism in America* (Berkeley: University of California Press, 2011), 10.

1. DEFENDING PRIVILEGE

1. DEFENDING PRIVILEGE

1. Huda Tabrez, "Four Workers Beaten Up in India for Eating Meat," *Gulf News*, June 1, 2019, https://gulfnews.com/world/asia/india/four-workers-beaten-up-in-india-for-eating-meat-1.64325346.
2. Vidhi Doshi, "To Protest Modi, These Indians Are Cooking Beef in Public," *Washington Post*, June 6, 2017, https://www.washingtonpost.com/world/asia_pacific/protests-against-the-governments-anti-beef-laws-spread-in-india/2017/06/05/8aa05dfc-489e-11e7-bcde-624ad94170ab_story.html.
3. Mostafa Salem, Pierre Bairin, Chris Liakos, Nadine Schmidt, and Sarah Dean, "Calls to Boycott French Products Grow in Muslim World After Macron Backs Mohammed Cartoons," *CNN*, October 27, 2020, https://www.cnn.com/2020/10/26/europe/france-boycott-muslim-countries-macron-intl/index.html.
4. Khader Abu-Seif, "Seeds of Hope? Arab Tahini Maker's Backing for LGBTQ Rights in Israel Shows Change Is Underway," *Haaretz*, June 13, 2020, https://www.haaretz.com/opinion/.premium-arab-israeli-tahini-maker-s-support-of-lgbtq-hotline-is-historic-moment-1.8988273.
5. Magda Teter, *Blood Libel: On The Trail of an Antisemitic Myth* (Cambridge, MA: Harvard University Press, 2020).
6. Bill Schutt, *Cannibalism: A Perfectly Natural History* (Chapel Hill: Algonquin, 2017).
7. Stefano Pivato, *I comunisti mangiano i bambini. Storia di una leggenda* (Bologna: Il Mulino, 2015).
8. Jumana Manna, "Where Nature Ends and Settlements Begin," *E-Flux Journal* 113, November 2020, https://www.e-flux.com/journal/113/360006/where-nature-ends-and-settlements-begin/.
9. Rabea Eghbariah, "The Criminalization of Za'atar and Akkoub: On Edible Plants in Palestinian Cuisine and Israeli Plant Protection Laws" (Hebrew), *Law, Society, and Culture Series* (2017): 497–533.
10. https://www.independent.co.uk/news/world/middle-east/israel-palestine-wine-vineyards-west-bank-psagot-settlement-eu-a8959301.html.
11. Bel Trew, "Grapes of Wrath: How Wine Could Bottle the Israeli-Palestinian Peace Process," *Independent*, June 16, 2019, https://www.trtworld.com/magazine/drunk-on-power-pompeo-approves-settlement-winery-as-made-in-israel-41654.

1. DEFENDING PRIVILEGE

12. Mike Shahanan, "Media Perceptions and Portrayals of Pastoralists in Kenya, India and China, in *The End of Desertification?*, ed. Roy Behnke and Michael Mortimore (Heidelberg: Springer, 2016): 407–25.
13. Tobias Hagmann and Alemmaya Mulugeta, "Pastoral Conflicts and State-Building in the Ethiopian Lowlands," *Africa Spectrum* 43, no. 1 (2008): 19–37.
14. Fekadu Beyene, "Natural Resource Conflict Analysis Among Pastoralists in Southern Ethiopia," *Journal of Peacebuilding and Development* 12, no. 1 (2017): 19–33.
15. Bamlaku Tadesse, Fekadu Beyene, Workneh Kassa, and Richard Wentzell, "The Dynamics of (Agro) Pastoral Conflicts in Eastern Ethiopia," *Ethiopian Journal of the Social Sciences and Humanities* 11, no. 1 (2015): 29–60.
16. Asnake Kefale, *Federalism and Ethnic Conflict in Ethiopia* (London: Routledge, 2013).
17. Ashwaq Masoodi, "A Story of Culinary Apartheid," *Mint*, September 16, 2016, https://www.livemint.com/Leisure/wJzDhGEE4csaX2BjhjHMsL/A-story-of-culinary-apartheid.html.
18. Soutik Biswas, "Is India's Ban on Cattle Slaughter 'Food Fascism?'" *BBC News*, June 2, 2017, https://www.bbc.com/news/world-asia-india-40116811.
19. "India Supreme Court Suspends Cattle Slaughter Ban," *BBC News*, July 11, 2017, https://www.bbc.com/news/world-asia-india-40565457.
20. APEDA, *Buffalo Meat*, http://apeda.gov.in/apedawebsite/SubHead_Products/Buffalo_Meat.htm.
21. Dolly Kikon, "The Politics of Dog Meat Ban in Nagaland," *Hindu*, July 14, 2020, https://frontline.thehindu.com/the-nation/the-politics-of-dog-meat-ban-in-nagaland/article32082833.ece/amp/?__twitter_impression=true.
22. "Citizenship Amendment Bill: India's New 'Anti-Muslim' Law Explained," *BBC*, December 11, 2019, https://www.bbc.com/news/world-asia-india-50670393.
23. "Mięsny problem Polaków" (magazine cover), *Newsweek*, July 8, 2019, https://adn-pro.fr/52525461b7126ef001f445ceaec7d8fe/magazine/newsweek-polska-8-lipca-2019.
24. "Kto chce nam zakazać jedzenia mięsa?! Nowe szaleństwo lewicy," *Do Rzeczy*, October 13, 2019, https://dorzeczy.pl/kraj/117113/do-rzeczy-nr-42-kto-chce-nam-zakazac-jedzenia-miesa.html.

1. DEFENDING PRIVILEGE

25. PAP, "Waszczykowski w niemieckiej gazecie: Nie chcemy świata złożonego z rowerzystów i wegetarian," *Newsweek*, April 1, 2016, https://www.newsweek.pl/polska/witold-waszczykowski-wywiad-dla-bild-rowerzysci-i-wegetarianie/88ojm5h.
26. "Robak na talerzu: kuchenne rewolucje" (magazin cover), March–April 2018, https://www.ksiegarnia.poloniachristiana.pl/produkt,polonia-christiana-nr-61,594.html.
27. Emily Crane, "How Biden's Climate Plan Could Limit You to Eat Just One Burger a MONTH, Cost $3.5K aYear per Person in Taxes, Force You to Spend $55K on an Electric Car and 'Crush' American Jobs," *Daily Mail*, April 22, 2021, https://www.dailymail.co.uk/news/article-9501565/How-Bidens-climate-plan-affect-everyday-Americans.html.
28. "Kudlow: Biden's Green New Deal Means No Meat for the 4th of July, Have Grilled Brussels Sprouts Instead," *Fox Business*, April 23 2021, https://www.foxbusiness.com/media/kudlow-bidens-climate-plan-means-no-meat-for-the-4th-of-july-have-grilled-brussel-sprouts-instead.
29. Jack Brewster, "Fox News Apologizes for Airing Misleading Graphic Accusing Biden of Wanting to Curb Meat Consumption," *Forbes*, April 26 2021, https://www.forbes.com/sites/jackbrewster/2021/04/26/fox-news-apologizes-for-airing-misleading-graphic-accusing-biden-of-wanting-to-curb-meat-consumption/?sh=5d2a8b924392.
30. Masami Iwasaki-Goodman, "Transmitting Ainu Traditional Food Knowledge from Mothers to Their Daughters," *Maternal and Child Nutrition* 12, no. S# (2017): e12555.
31. Ellie Cobb, "Japan's Unknown Indigenous Cuisine," *BBC*, August 11, 2020, https://www.bbc.com/travel/article/20200810-japans-unknown-indigenous-cuisine.
32. Devon A. Mihesuah and Elizabeth Hoover, foreword by Winona LaDuke, *Indigenous Food Sovereignty in the United States: Restoring Cultural Knowledge, Protecting Environments, and Regaining Health* (Norman: University of Oklahoma Press, 2019).
33. "Unsustainable Cattle Ranching," *WWF*, https://wwf.panda.org/discover/knowledge_hub/where_we_work/amazon/amazon_threats/unsustainable_cattle_ranching/?.
34. The Sioux Chef, https://sioux-chef.com/about/.
35. Judith Carney, *Black Rice: The African Origins of Rice Cultivation in the Americas* (Cambridge, MA: Harvard University Press, 2001).

36. Jane Fajans, *Brazilian Food: Race, Class, and Identity in Regional Cuisines* (Oxford: Berg, 2012).
37. Adrian Miller, *The President's Kitchen Cabinet: The Story of the African Americans Who Have Fed Our First Families, from the Washingtons to the Obamas* (Chapel Hill: University of North Carolina Press, 2017); Toni Tipton-Martin, *The Jemima Code: Two Centuries of African American Cookbooks* (Austin: University of Texas Press, 2015).
38. Jennifer Jensen Wallach, ed., *Dethroning the Deceitful Porkchop: Rethinking African American Foodways from Slavery to Obama* (Fayetteville: University of Arkansas Press, 2015); Psyche Williams-Forson, *Building Houses Out of Chicken Legs: Black Women, Food, and Power* (Chapel Hill: University of North Carolina Press, 2006).
39. Doris Witt, *Black Hunger: Food and the Politics of U.S. Identity* (New York: Oxford University Press, 1999).
40. Jessica Harris, *Beyond Gumbo: Creole Fusion Food from the Atlantic Rim* (New York: Simon and Schuster, 2012).

2. TOWARD A BETTER FUTURE

1. Slow Food Pavilion—Milan Expo 2015 / Herzog & de Meuron, Archdaily.com, http://www.archdaily.com/634043/slow-food-pavilion-herzog-and-de-meuron.
2. Slow Food, "Good, Clean, and Fair: The Slow Food Manifesto for Quality," 2015, https://www.slowfood.com/wp-content/uploads/2015/07/Manifesto_Quality_ENG.pdf.
3. Stefano Rizzato, "Expo, McDonald's risponde a Petrini: L'ideologia non sfamerà il Pianeta," *La Stampa*, May 20, 2015, http://www.lastampa.it/2015/05/20/societa/expo2015/expo-mcdonalds-risponde-a-petrini-lideologia-non-sfamer-il-pianeta-YbQsDCkDK3oSrK9uNDbnZM/pagina.html.
4. Clare Midgley, "Slave Sugar Boycotts, Female Activism, and the Domestic Base of British Anti-slavery Culture," *Slavery and Abolition* 17, no. 3 (1996): 137–62.
5. Julie L. Holcomb, *Moral Commerce: Quakers and the Transatlantic Boycott of the Slave Labor Economy* (Ithaca, NY: Cornell University Press, 2016).
6. Jethro Mullen and Mark Morgenstein, "Anti-whaling activists Say They Were Attacked by Japanese Ships," CNN, February 25, 2013, https://www.cnn.com/2013/02/20/world/asia/australia-japan-whaling/index.html.

2. TOWARD A BETTER FUTURE

7. International Whaling Commission, *Commercial Whaling,* "https://iwc.int/commercial.
8. https://wwf.panda.org/discover/knowledge_hub/endangered_species/cetaceans/cetaceans/iwc/iwc_successes_failures/?.
9. Elizabeth Claire Alberts, "481 and Counting: Norway's Whaling Catch Hits Four-Year High," Mongabay.com, August 27, 2020, https://news.mongabay.com/2020/08/481-and-counting-norways-whaling-catch-hits-four-year-high/; Ariella Simke, "Iceland to Stop Killing Whales in 2020, Choosing to Watch Them Instead," Forbes.com, May 10, 2020, https://www.forbes.com/sites/ariellasimke/2020/05/10/iceland-to-stop-killing-whales-in-2020-choosing-to-watch-them-instead/?sh=7514ed4e3d0d.
10. Reuters, "Brazil Amazon Deforestation Hits Twelve-Year High Under Bolsonaro," *New York Times,* November 30, 2020, https://www.nytimes.com/2020/11/30/world/americas/brazil-amazon-rainforest-deforestation.html.
11. Survival International, *What Brazil's President, Jair Bolsonaro, Has Said About Brazil's Indigenous Peoples,* https://www.survivalinternational.org/articles/3540-Bolsonaro.
12. Matin Qaim, Kibrom T. Sibhatu, Hermanto Siregar, and Ingo Grass, "Environmental, Economic, and Social Consequences of the Oil Palm Boom," *Annual Review of Resource Economics* 12 (2020): 321–44.
13. Philip McMichael, "The Land Grab and Corporate Food Regime Restructuring," *Journal of Peasant Studies* 39, no. 3–4 (2012): 681–701.
14. Alyshia Gálvez, *Eating NAFTA Trade, Food Policies, and the Destruction of Mexico* (Los Angeles: University of California Press, 2018).
15. Elizabeth Fitting, "Cultures of Corn and Anti-GM Activism in Mexico and Colombia," in *Food Activism: Agency, Democracy and Economy,* ed. Carole Counihan and Valeria Siniscalchi (London: Bloomsbury, 2014), 175–92.
16. Filippo Tosatto, "Friuli, raid contro campo Ogm: Scoppia la lite fra Zaia e Galan," *La Repubblica,* August 10, 2010, https://www.repubblica.it/politica/2010/08/10/news/ogm_zaia_galan-6196865/.
17. Mike Adams, "Hungary Torches 500 Hectares of GM Corn to Eradicate GMOs from Food Supply," *Natural News,* May 29, 2013, https://www.naturalnews.com/040525_Hungary_GM_corn_burning_fields.html#ixzz2XKaTWwJg.
18. K. V. Venkatasubramanian, "Illegally Grown GM Aubergines Highlight India's Continuing Ambivalence to Transgenic Crops," *Chemistry World,* May 30, 2019, https://www.chemistryworld.com/news/illegally-grown

-gm-aubergines-highlight-indias-continuing-ambivalence-to-transgenic-crops/3010557.article.
19. K. S. Jayaraman, "Illegal Seeds Overtake India's Cotton Fields," *Nature Biotechnology* 22, no. 11 (2004): 1333–34.
20. Branden Born and Mark Purcell, "Avoiding the Local Trap: Scale and Food Systems in Planning Research," *Journal of Planning Education and Research* 26, no. 2 (2006): 195–207.
21. Tanya Denckla Cobb, *Reclaiming Our Food: How the Grassroots Food Movement Is Changing the Way We Eat* (North Adams, MA: Storey, 2011).
22. Alison Hope Alkon and Julian Agyeman, *Cultivating Food Justice: Race, Class, and Sustainability* (Cambridge, MA: MIT Press, 2011); Kristin Reynolds and Nevin Cohen, *Beyond the Kale: Urban Agriculture and Social Justice Activism in New York City* (Athens: University of Georgia Press, 2016).
23. Ashanté M. Reese and Hanna Garth, *Black Food Matters: Racial Justice in the Wake of Food Justice* (Minneapolis: University of Minnesota Press, 2020).
24. U.S. Food Sovereignty Alliance, "Food Sovereignty," http://usfoodsovereigntyalliance.org/what-is-food-sovereignty/.
25. Nyéléni Forum, "Declaration of Nyeleni," *Nyeleni.org*, February 27, 2007, https://nyeleni.org/spip.php?article290.
26. Jack Kloppenburg, "Re-purposing the Master's Tools: The Open Source Seed Initiative and the Struggle for Seed Sovereignty," *Journal of Peasant Studies* 41, no. 6 (2014): 1225–46.

3. FOOD AND IDENTITY

1. The literature on the relationship between food and identity is quite extensive. We can mention Steffan Igor Ayora-Diaz, ed., *Cultural Politics of Food, Taste, and Identity: A Global Perspective* (London: Bloomsbury, 2021); Elizabeth Capaldi, ed., *Why We Eat What We Eat: The Psychology of Eating* (Washington, DC: American Psychological Association, 1996); Patricia Caplan, ed., *Food, Health, and Identity* (London: Routledge, 1997); Allison James, Anne Trine Kjørholt, and Vebjørg Tingstad, *Children, Food, and Identity in Everyday Life* (New York: Palgrave Macmillan, 2009); Katheryn C Twiss, *The Archaeology of Food and Identity* (Carbondale, IL: Southern Illinois University Press, 2007);. Much research has explored the role of food in the historical formation of identities, including Ken Albala and Trudy Eden, *Food and Faith in Christian Culture* (New York:

3. FOOD AND IDENTITY

Columbia University Press, 2011); Stephen Mennell, *All Manners of Food: Eating and Taste in England and France from the Middle Ages to the Present* (Urbana: University of Illinois Press, 1996), Peter Scholliers, ed., *Food, Drink, and Identity: Cooking, Eating, and Drinking in Europe Since the Middle Ages* (Oxford: Berg, 2001).

2. Lucy M. Long, ed., *Culinary Tourism* (Lexington: University Press of Kentucky, 2003).
3. Lisa M. Heldke, *Exotic Appetites: Ruminations of a Food Adventurer* (London: Routledge, 2003).
4. bell hooks, "Eating the Other: Desire and Resistance," in *Black Looks: Race and Representation* (Boston: South End, 1992), 21–39.
5. Claude Fischler, "Food, Self, and Identity," *Social Science Information* 27, no 2 (1988): 275–92.
6. Claude Lévi-Strauss, *The Origin of Table Manners* (New York: Harper-Collins, 1978), 471.
7. Eric Hobsbawm, "Introduction: Inventing Tradition," in *The Invention of Tradition*, ed. Eric Hobsbawm and Terence Ranger (Cambridge: Cambridge University Press, 1983), 1.
8. Ronda Brulotte and Michael Di Giovine, eds., *Edible Identities: Food as Cultural Heritage* (Farnham: Ashgate, 2014); Ilaria Porciani, ed., *Food Heritage and Nationalism in Europe* (New York: Routledge, 2019).
9. Rodney Harrison, *Heritage: Critical Approaches* (New York: Routledge, 2013), 69.
10. Dallen Timothy, *Heritage Cuisines: Traditions, Identities, and Tourism* (New York: Taylor and Francis, 2016).
11. Barbara Kirshenblatt-Gimblett, "Theorizing Heritage," *Ethnomusicology* 39, no 3 (1995): 367–80.
12. Emily J. H. Contois and Zenia Kish, eds., *Food Instagram: Identity, Influence, and Negotiation* (Champaign: University of Illinois Press, 2022); Jonatan Leer and Stinne Gunder Strøm Krogager, *Research Methods in Digital Food Studies* (London: Routledge: 2021).
13. Massimo Montanari, *Il mito delle origini: Breve storia degli spaghetti al pomodoro* (Bari: Laterza, 2019).
14. Rekha Dixit, "Farming Is Indian, not Iranian," *Week*, November 1, 2020, https://www.theweek.in/health/more/2020/10/23/farming-is-Indian-not-Iranian.html.
15. Jean-Pierre Poulain, "The Sociology of Gastronomic Decolonization," in *The Gaze of the West: Framings of the East Shanta*, ed. Shanta Nair-Venugopal (New York: Palgrave Macmillan, 2011), 218–32.

4. FOOD AND POWER

16. Considerable research has been conducted on food and authenticity, for example, Kaitland M. Byrd, *Real Southern Barbecue: Constructing Authenticity in Southern Food Culture* (Lanham, MD: Lexington, 2019); Kaelyn Stiles, Özlem Altıok, and Michael M. Bell, "The Ghosts of Taste: Food and the Cultural Politics of Authenticity," *Agriculture and Human Values* 28 (2011): 225–36; Fabio Parasecoli, "The Invention of Authentic Italian Food: Narratives, Rhetoric, and Media," in Roberta Sassatelli, ed., *Italians and Food* (Basingstoke: Palgrave McMillan, 2019), 17–42; Matthew Strohl, "On Culinary Authenticity," *Journal of Aesthetics and Art Criticism* 77, no. 2 (2019): 157–67.
17. Joseph Pine II and James H. Gilmore, *The Experience Economy: Work Is Theater and Every Business a Stage* (Cambridge, MA: Harvard Business School Press, 1999).

4. FOOD AND POWER

1. Antonia Mortensen and Laura Smith-Spark, "Poland's Biggest Protests in Decades Stand Against Abortion Ban," *CNN*, October 31 2020, https://www.cnn.com/2020/10/31/europe/poland-abortion-protests-scli-intl/index.html.
2. Jackie Flynn Mogensen, "The Million MAGA March Hashtag Has Been Taken Over by Images of Pancakes," *Mother Jones*, November 14, 2020, https://www.motherjones.com/food/2020/11/the-million-maga-march-hashtag-has-been-taken-over-by-images-of-pancakes/.
3. Will Bedingfield, "K-Pop Stans Took on Trump in Tulsa, Now They're After the White House," *Wired*, June 24, 2020, https://www.wired.co.uk/article/k-pop-trump.
4. PTI, "BJP Attacks Delhi Government for Spiralling Onion Prices." *Economic Times*, October 22, 2013, https://economictimes.indiatimes.com/news/politics-and-nation/bjp-attacks-delhi-government-for-spiralling-onion-prices/articleshow/24553941.cms?from=mdr.
5. Rajendra Jadhav and Mayank Bhardwaj, "Collapse in India's Onion Prices Could Leave Modi Smarting in Election," *Reuters*, December 27, 2018, https://www.reuters.com/article/uk-india-election-onions-insight-idINKCN1OR03O; Rohit Inani, "The Onion Bomb and Hindu Nationalism," *NewLines*, December 16, 2020, https://newlinesmag.com/reportage/the-onion-bomb-and-hindu-nationalism/.
6. Lauren Frayer, "India's Farmer Protests: Why Are They So Angry?," *NPR*, March 2, 2021, https://www.npr.org/sections/goatsandsoda/2021/03/02/971293844/indias-farmer-protests-why-are-they-so-angry.

4. FOOD AND POWER

7. Emily Schmall, Karan Deep Singh and Sameer Yasir, "In Rare Show of Weakness, Modi Bows to India's Farmers," *New York Times*, November 18, 2021, https://www.nytimes.com/2021/11/18/world/asia/india-farmers-modi.html.
8. Letter of Sir Sayyid Ahmed Khan to Sir John Kaye, in Salim ud-Din Quraishi, ed., *Asbab-e baghavat-e Hind* (Lahore: Sang-e Meel, 1997), 122–27, http://www.columbia.edu/itc/mealac/pritchett/00urdu/asbab/bijnor/app05_letter1869.html.
9. Betsy Kuhn, *The Force Born of Truth: Mohandas Gandhi and the Salt March, India, 1930* (Minneapolis: Twenty-First Century, 2011).
10. "The Cost of Food: Facts and Figures," *BBC News*, October 16, 2008, http://news.bbc.co.uk/2/hi/7284196.stm.
11. Patrick Westhoff, *The Economics of Food: How Feeding and Fueling the Planet Affects Food Prices* (Upper Saddle River, NJ: Pearson Education, 2010).
12. Philip McMichael, "A Food Regime Genealogy," *Journal of Peasant Studies* 36, no. 1 (2009): 139–69.
13. Nico Colombant, "UN Condemns al-Shabab Raids and Humanitarian Aid Ban," *VOA News*, November 27, 2011, https://www.voanews.com/africa/un-condemns-al-shabab-raids-and-humanitarian-aid-ban.
14. Lynzy Billing, "Duterte's Response to the Coronavirus: 'Shoot Them Dead,'" *Foreign Policy*, April 16, 2020, https://foreignpolicy.com/2020/04/16/duterte-philippines-coronavirus-response-shoot-them-dead/.
15. "Campaign Digest | Obama Elaborates on Arugula Sound Bite," *Seattle Times*, October 7, 2007, https://www.seattletimes.com/seattle-news/politics/campaign-digest-obama-elaborates-on-arugula-sound-bite/.
16. Michael M. Grynbaum, "A Fork? De Blasio's Way of Eating Pizza Is Mocked," *New York Times*, January 10, 2014, https://www.nytimes.com/2014/01/11/nyregion/de-blasio-skewered-for-eating-pizza-with-utensils.html.
17. Matthew Schwartz, "Feast Fit for a Burger King: Trump Serves Fast Food to College Football Champs," *NPR*, January 15, 2019, https://www.npr.org/2019/01/15/685416350/feast-fit-for-a-burger-king-trump-serves-fast-food-to-college-football-champs.
18. Jukka Gronow, *Caviar with Champagne: Common Luxury and the Ideals of the Good Life in Stalin's Russia* (Oxford: Berg, 2003); Albena Shkodrova, *Communist Gourmet: The Curious Story of Food in the People's Republic of Bulgaria* (Budapest: Central European University Press, 2021).

5. FOOD, NATIONS, AND NATIONALISM

19. Anne Applebaum, *Red Famine: Stalin's War on Ukraine* (New York: Anchor, 2018).
20. Frank Dikötter, *Mao's Great Famine: The History of China's Most Devastating Catastrophe, 1958–62* (London: Bloomsbury, 2010).
21. Tiago Saraiva, *Fascist Pigs: Technoscientific Organisms and the History of Fascism* (Cambridge, MA: MIT Press, 2016).
22. Antonio Gramsci, *The Antonio Gramsci Reader*, ed. David Forgacs (New York: New York University Press, 2000).
23. Carol Helstosky, "Fascist Food Politics: Mussolini's Policy of Alimentary Sovereignty," *Journal of Modern Italian Studies* 9, no. 1 (2004): 1–26.

5. FOOD, NATIONS, AND NATIONALISM

1. Gambero Rosso, "30 anni di Gambero Rosso. Correva l'anno: 2011," Gambero Rosso, December 15, 2016, https://www.gamberorosso.it/uncategorized/30-anni-di-gambero-rosso-correva-l-anno-2011/.
2. Ministerstwo Rolnictwa i Rozwoju Wsi, "Kanon kuchni polskiej—zapraszamy do konsultacji," *Gov.pl*, September 2, 2019, https://www.gov.pl/web/rolnictwo/kanon-kuchni-polskiej—zapraszamy-do-konsultacji.
3. Atsuko Ichijo and Ronald Ranta, *Food, National Identity, and Nationalism* (New York: Palgrave MacMillan, 2016).
4. Adam Folvarčný and Lubomír Kopeček, "Which Conservatism? The Identity of the Polish Law and Justice Party," *Politics in Central Europe* 16, no. 1 (2020): 159–88; David Clarke and Paweł Duber, "Polish Cultural Diplomacy and Historical Memory: The Case of the Museum of the Second World War in Gdańsk," *International Journal of Politics, Culture, and Society* 33 (2020): 49–66.
5. Michaela deSoucey, "Gastronationalism: Food Traditions and Authenticity Politics in the European Union," *American Sociological Review* 75, no. 3 (2010): 432–55, 433.
6. Richard Wilk, *Home Cooking in the Global Village: Caribbean Food from Buccaneers to Ecotourists* (Oxford: Berg, 2006); Richard Wilk, ed., *Fast Food/Slow Food: The Cultural Economy of the Global Food System* (Lanham: Altamira, 2006).
7. Jason Edwards, "O, the Roast Beef of Old England! Brexit and Gastronationalism," *Political Quarterly* 90, no. 4 (2019): 629–36, 630.
8. Edwards, 631.

5. FOOD, NATIONS, AND NATIONALISM

9. Benedict Anderson, *Imagined Communities: Reflections on the Origin and Spread of Nationalism* (London: Verso, 1991).
10. Michael Billig, *Banal Nationalism* (London: Sage, 1996).
11. Michel Foucault, "The Birth of Biopolitics," in *Ethics: Subjectivity and Truth*, ed. Paul Rabinow (New York: New Press, 1997), 73–79.
12. Alfred Crosby, *Ecological Imperialism: The Biological Expansion of Europe, 900–1900* (Cambridge: Cambridge University Press, 2004); Ulrike Kirchberger and Brett M. Bennett, eds., *Environments of Empire: Networks and Agents of Ecological Change* (Chapel Hill: University of North Carolina Press, 2020).
13. Fabio Parasecoli, "World Food: The Age of Empire c. 1800–1920, " in Martin Bruegel, ed., *A Cultural History of Food: In the Age of Empire* (London: Berg, 2012), 199–208.
14. Nicholas Tošaj, "Finding France in Flour: Communicating Colonialism in French Indochina Through Bread," in Cecilia Leong-Salobir, ed., *Routledge Handbook of Food in Asia* (London: Routledge, 2019), 29–38.
15. Jonathan Robins, "'Imbibing the Lesson of Defiance': Oil Palms and Alcohol in Colonial Ghana, 1900–40," *Environmental History* 23, no. 2 (2018): 293–317.
16. National Research Council, *Lost Crops of Africa*, vol. 1: *Grains* (Washington, DC: National Academies Press, 1996).
17. Fundació Institut Català de la Cuina, *Corpus del patrimoni culinari català* (Barcelona: RBA La Magrana, 2016).
18. "Biblioteca básica de cocinas tradicionales de Colombia," *mincultura.gov.co*, https://mincultura.gov.co/areas/patrimonio/Paginas/bibliotecas-de-cocinas.aspx.
19. Raúl Matta, "Mexico's Ethnic Culinary Heritage and Cocineras Tradicionales (Traditional Female Cooks)," *Food and Foodways* 27, no. 3 (2019): 211–31.
20. Renata Hryciuk, "La Alquimista de los Sabores: Gastronomic Heritage, Gender, and the Tourist Imaginary in Mexico," *Revista del CESLA* 24 (2019): 75–100.
21. Raúl Matta, "Food Incursions Into Global Heritage: Peruvian Cuisine's Slippery Road to UNESCO," *Social Anthropology* 24, no. 3 (2016): 338–52.
22. Arturo Wallace, "Contrastes, racismo, gastronomía . . . 8 claves para entender mejor a Perú y los peruanos," *BBC News*, December 9, 2016, https://www.bbc.com/mundo/noticias-america-latina-38094026.

6. FOOD AND DIPLOMACY

23. Catarina Passidomo, "'Our' Culinary Heritage: Obscuring Inequality by Celebrating Diversity in Peru and the U.S. South," *Humanity and Society* 41, no. 4 (2017): 427–45, 427.
24. Arjun Appadurai, "How to Make a National Cuisine: Cookbooks in Contemporary India," *Comparative Studies in Society and History* 30, no. 1 (1988.): 3–24.
25. "Minister Advocates Nigerian Food as Tourism Products," *This Day*, June 23, 2021, https://www.thisdaylive.com/index.php/2021/06/23/minister-advocates-nigerian-food-as-tourism-products/.
26. Lopè Ariyo, *Hibiscus* (New York: HarperCollins, 2017); Ozoz Sokoh, "Six (6) Ways to Grow Food Tourism in Nigeria," *Kitchen Butterfly*, May 8, 2017, https://www.kitchenbutterfly.com/2017/six-6-ways-to-grow-food-tourism-in-nigeria/.
27. Nancy Silverman, *Nigerian Recipe Book: A Beginner's Guide to Authentic Nigerian* (self-published, 2019).
28. Sidney Mintz, *Tasting Food, Tasting Freedom: Excursions Into Eating, Culture, and the Past* (Boston: Beacon, 1996), 106–24.
29. Robin Cook, "Robin Cook's Chicken Tikka Masala Speech," *Guardian*, April 19, 2001, https://www.theguardian.com/world/2001/apr/19/race.britishidentity.

6. FOOD AND DIPLOMACY

1. "Thailand's Gastro-Diplomacy," *Economist*, February 21, 2002, Econohttps://www.economist.com/asia/2002/02/21/thailands-gastro-diplomacy.
2. Mary Jo A. Pham, "Food as Communication: A Case Study of South Korea's Gastrodiplomacy," *Journal of International Service* 22, no. 1 (2013): 5, https://thediplomatistdotcom.files.wordpress.com/2013/01/jis-spring-2013-issue-gastrodiplomacy.pdf.
3. Shannon Haugh, "Letter from the Editor," *Public Diplomacy Magazine* (2014): 9, quoted in Catarina Passidomo, "'Our' Culinary Heritage: Obscuring Inequality by Celebrating Diversity in Peru and the U.S. South," *Humanity and Society* 41, no. 4 (2017): 427–45, 431.
4. Paul Rockower, "Korean Tacos and Kimchi Diplomacy," *USC Public Diplomacy*, March 25, 2010, https://www.uscpublicdiplomacy.org/blog/korean-tacos-and-kimchi-diplomacy.

6. FOOD AND DIPLOMACY

5. Cita Stelzer, *Dinner with Churchill: Policy-Making at the Dinner Table* (Cambridge: Pegasus, 2013).
6. Margaret MacMillan, *Nixon and Mao: The Week That Changed the World* (New York: Random House, 2008).
7. Richard Wilk, *Home Cooking in the Global Village: Caribbean Food from Buccaneers to Ecotourists* (Oxford: Berg, 2006), 167–68.
8. Saubhadra Chatterji, "At Banquet for Donald Trump, Salmon Tikka, Raan Ali-shan to Mark Cultural Fusion," *Hindustan Times*, February 25, 2020, https://www.hindustantimes.com/india-news/at-banquet-dinner-for-donald-trump-salmon-tikka-raan-ali-shan-to-mark-cultural-fusion/story-RTYB9RTnmw73bheprg3pYP.html.
9. Tim Wyatt, "Trump and His Entourage Fail to Eat Anything from Special Vegetarian Menu Prepared for Them on India Trip," *Independent*, February 25, 2020, https://www.independent.co.uk/news/world/asia/donald-trump-india-vegetarian-menu-samosa-broccoli-modi-gandhi-ashram-a9356666.html.
10. https://www.youtube.com/watch?v=8joXlwKMkrk.
11. Raúl Matta, "República gastronómica y país de cocineros: Comida, política, medios y una nueva idea de nación para el Perú," *Revista Colombiana de Antropología* 50, no. 2 (2014): 15–40.
12. Eric C. Rath, *Japan Cuisines: Food, Place and Identity* (London: Reaktion, 2016).
13. Chung Min-uck, "Chinese Upset in Kimchi Cabbage Row," *Korea Times*, May 4, 2012, http://www.koreatimes.co.kr/www/news/nation/2012/05/113_110298.html.
14. Codex Alimentarius, *Standard for Kimchi: CXS 223-2001, Adopted in 2001. Amended in 2017* (Rome: Food and Agriculture Organization of the United Nations, 2017).
15. Youmi Kim and Mike Ives, "Is China Laying Claim to Kimchi, Too? Some South Koreans Think So," *New York Times*, December 1, 2020, https://www.nytimes.com/2020/12/01/world/asia/south-korea-china-kimchi-paocai.html.

7. NATIONAL PRODUCTS IN THE GLOBAL MARKET

1. Reihi Yoshida, "Ten Sick After Eating Tainted 'Gyoza' from China," *Japan Times*, January 31, 2008, https://www.japantimes.co.jp/news/2008/01/31/national/10-sick-after-eating-tainted-gyoza-from-china/.

7. NATIONAL PRODUCTS IN THE GLOBAL MARKET

2. Yanzhong Huang, "The 2008 Milk Scandal Revisited," *Forbes*, July 16, 2014, https://www.forbes.com/sites/yanzhonghuang/2014/07/16/the-2008-milk-scandal-revisited/?sh=ea9d99c4105b.
3. Wu Jiao, "Checks on Animal Feed 'Tightened,'" *China Daily*, November 1, 2008, http://www.chinadaily.com.cn/china/2008-11/01/content_7164471.htm.
4. Karita Kan and Samson Yuen, "Visceral Politics Across the Strait: Food and Risk in China-Taiwan Relations," *China Information* 32, no. 3 (2018): 443–62.
5. Katarzyna Cwiertka, *Modern Japanese Cuisine: Food, Power, and National Identity*, (London: Reaktion, 2006).
6. Eric Rath and Stephanie Assman, eds., *Japanese Foodways, Past and Present*, (Urbana: University of Illinois Press, 2010).
7. Nancy Rosenberger, "Global Food Terror in Japan: Media Shaping Risk Perception, the Nation, and Women," *Ecology of Food and Nutrition* 48, no. 4 (2009): 237–62.
8. Tine Walravens, "Recalibrating Risk Through Media: Two Cases of Intentional Food Poisoning in Japan," *Food and Foodways* 27, nos. 1–2 (2019): 74–97, DOI: 10.1080/07409710.2019.1568852.
9. Alessandro Gorgiutti, "Foreign Food Is Toxic," *Libero*, October 13, 2019, 1 and 3.
10. Vincent Wood, "Italian Far-Right Leader Salvini Swears Off Eating Nutella After Finding Out It Contains Turkish Nuts," *Independent*, December 6, 2019, https://www.independent.co.uk/news/world/europe/salvini-nutella-italy-turkish-hazelnuts-league-renzi-a9236166.html.
11. SkyTG24, "Parlamento europeo, show dell'eurodeputato Ciocca che lancia cioccolato turco. VIDEO," *Sky.it*, October 24, 2019, https://tg24.sky.it/mondo/2019/10/24/parlamento-europeo-leghista-ciocca-cioccolato-turco-video.
12. "Farmers Hand Out Free Milk in Paris in Price Protest," *Reuters*, September 22, 2009, https://www.reuters.com/article/us-france-milk/farmers-hand-out-free-milk-in-paris-in-price-protest-idUSTRE58L30W20090922.
13. John Lichfield, "French Farmers Block Roads in Protest at Huge Drop in Milk and Pork Prices Following Russian Trade Sanctions," *Independent*, February 15, 2016, https://www.independent.co.uk/news/world/europe/french-farmers-block-roads-protest-huge-drop-milk-and-pork-prices-following-russian-trade-sanctions-a6875581.html.

7. NATIONAL PRODUCTS IN THE GLOBAL MARKET

14. "China Punishes Australia for Promoting an Inquiry Into Covid-19," *Economist*, May 23, 2020, https://www.economist.com/asia/2020/05/21/china-punishes-australia-for-promoting-an-inquiry-into-covid-19.
15. "Russia Approves Higher Wheat Export Tax from March 1," *Reuters*, January 26, 2021, https://www.reuters.com/article/russia-wheat-exports/russia-approves-higher-wheat-export-tax-from-march-1-idUSR4N2JA0oU.
16. Alina Kühnel, "Germany Drafts Romanian Farm Labor for Coronavirus Pandemic," *DW*, April 8, 2020, https://www.dw.com/en/germany-drafts-romanian-farm-labor-for-coronavirus-pandemic/a-53066735.
17. Maria Wilczek, "Poland Loosens Lockdown for Workers from Ukraine and Poles with Jobs in Germany," *Notes from Poland*, May 5, 2020, https://notesfrompoland.com/2020/05/05/poland-loosens-lockdown-for-workers-from-ukraine-and-poles-with-jobs-in-germany/.
18. Catherine Boudreau, "Trump Country Hit Hard by Chinese Tariffs," *Politico*, July 6, 2018, https://www.politico.com/story/2018/07/06/trump-china-tariffs-farmers-672103.
19. Wendong Zhang and Minghao Li, "Most US Farmers Remain Loyal to Trump Despite Pain from Trade Wars and COVID-19," *Conversation*, October 19, 2020, https://theconversation.com/most-us-farmers-remain-loyal-to-trump-despite-pain-from-trade-wars-and-covid-19-146535.
20. CNIEL, "#Fromagissons: appel collectif de la filière laitière pour une consommation solidaire de nos fromages de tradition partout en France," *Presse Filière Laitière*, April 15, 2020, https://presse.filiere-laitiere.fr/actualites/fromagissons-appel-collectif-de-la-filiere-laitiere-pour-une-consommation-solidaire-de-nos-fromages-de-tradition-partout-en-france-co B.C.-ef05e.html.
21. Samuel Petrequin, "Coronavirus: Belgians Urged to Eat More Fries to Save the Country's Beloved Potato Industry, *Stuff*, April 29, 2020, https://www.stuff.co.nz/world/europe/300000961/coronavirus-belgians-urged-to-eat-more-fries-to-save-the-countrys-beloved-potato-industry.
22. Aidan Fortune, "AHDB Launches Steak Night Campaign to Combat Drop in Eating Out," *Food Navigator*, April 13, 2020, https://www.foodnavigator.com/Article/2020/04/13/AHDB-launches-steak-night-campaign-to-combat-drop-in-eating-out.
23. Maria Wilczek, "Polish Government Publishes List of 'Unpatriotic' Firms Importing Milk from Other EU Countries," *Notes from Poland*, April 24, 2020, https://notesfrompoland.com/2020/04/24/polish-government

8. MIGRANT FOOD

-publishes-list-of-unpatriotic-firms-importing-milk-from-other-eu
-countries/.
24. Erik Sherman, "Here's the Crushing Truth About American Farmers Under Trump's Trade War," *Forbes*, December 27, 2019, https://www.forbes.com/sites/eriksherman/2019/12/27/trump-china-tariffs-farmers-subsidies/?sh=31fb76ee5b39.
25. Patrice Gaines, "USDA Issued Billions in Subsidies This Year: Black Farmers Are Still Waiting for Their Share," *NBC News*, October 28, 2020, https://www.nbcnews.com/news/nbcblk/usda-issued-billions-subsidies-year-black-farmers-are-still-waiting-n1245090.
26. Such short-term interventions add up to the vast subsidies that farmers already receive in high-income countries, which have been contentious on the international stage, whereas low- and middle-income countries do not have the means to sustain such policies or are prevented from doing so by international regulations. See Minju Kim and Hyo-Young Lee, "Looking Beyond the DOHA Negotiations: A Possible Reform of the WTO Agricultural Subsidies Rules," *Asian Journal of WTO and International Health Law and Policy* 12, no. 1 (2017): 171–200.
27. James Scott, "The Future of Agricultural Trade Governance in the World Trade Organization," *International Affairs* 93, no. 5 (2017): 1167–84.

8. MIGRANT FOOD

1. Marin Wagda, "Le couscous: Nouveau plat national du pays de France," *Hommes et Migrations* 1205 (1997): 142–43, https://www.persee.fr/doc/homig_1142-852x_1997_num_1205_1_2913.
2. Krystian Nowak, *Kebabistan: Rzecz o Polskim daniu narodowym* (Warsaw: Krytyka Polityczna, 2020).
3. Pierre Raffard, "The Doner Kebab, an Unlikely Symbol of European Identity," *pri.org*, May 15, 2019, https://www.pri.org/stories/2019-05-15/doner-kebab-unlikely-symbol-european-identity.
4. Nazareno Panichella, *Meridionali al Nord. Migrazioni interne e società italiana dal dopoguerra ad oggi* (Bologna: Il Mulino, 2014).
5. Tracy N. Poe, "The Origins of Soul Food in Black Urban Identity: Chicago, 1915–1947," *American Studies International* 37, no. 1 (1999): 4–33.
6. Ayixiamuguli Ayoufu, Degang Yang, and Dilshat Yimit, "Uyghur Food Culture," *Asia Pacific Journal of Clinical Nutrition* 26, no. 5 (2017): 764–68.

8. MIGRANT FOOD

7. Julie Cavignac Universidade, Maria Isabel Dantas, and Gabriela da Silva Sales Beltrão, "Comidas do sertão: uma leitura da história e da cultura," *Revista Ingesta* 1, no. 2 (2019): 213–14.
8. United Nations Population Division, "Urban Population," *World Bank*, https://data.worldbank.org/indicator/SP.URB.TOTL.IN.ZS.
9. Kristin Reynolds and Nevin Cohen, *Beyond the Kale: Urban Agriculture and Social Justice Activism in New York City* (Athens: University of Georgia Press, 2016).
10. "La Via Campesina Declaration on Migration and Rural Workers," viacampesina.org, April 2, 2015, https://viacampesina.org/en/la-via-campesina-declaration-on-migration-and-rural-workers/.
11. Noah Allison, "Immigrant Foodways: Restaurants, Street Food, and Ethnic Diversity in Queens, New York," Ph.D. diss., New School, 2020.
12. Hasia Diner, *Hungering for America: Italian, Irish, and Jewish Foodways in the Age of Migration* (Cambridge, MA: Harvard University Press, 2001).
13. Marcel Mauss, "Techniques of the Body," *Economy and Society* 2, no. 1 (1973): 70–85, 70.
14. David E. Sutton, *Remembrance of Repasts: An Anthropology of Food and Memory* (Oxford: Berg, 2001).
15. Simone Cinotto, *The Italian American Table: Food, Family, and Community in New York City* (Urbana: University of Illinois Press, 2013).
16. Elizabeth Zanoni, *Migrant Marketplaces: Food and Italians in North and South America* (Urbana: University of Illinois Press, 2018).
17. Ajay Bailey, "The Migrant Suitcase: Food, Belonging, and Commensality Among Indian Migrants in the Netherlands," *Appetite* 110 (March 2017): 51–60, DOI: https://doi.org/10.1016/j.appet.2016.12.013; Krishnendu Ray, *The Migrant's Table: Meals and Memories in Bengali-American Households* (Philadelphia: Temple University Press, 2004).
18. Anne J. Kershen, ed., *Food in the Migrant Experience* (London: Routledge, 2016).
19. James Farrer, "From Cooks to Chefs: Skilled Migrants in a Globalising Culinary Field," *Journal of Ethnic and Migration Studies* (2020), DOI: 10.1080/1369183X.2020.1731990.
20. Krishnendu Ray, *The Ethnic Restaurateur* (London: Bloomsbury, 2016).
21. Yong Chen, *The Story of Chinese Food in America* (New York: Columbia University Press, 2014).

9. CONTAGIONS

1. Ann H. Reid, Thomas G. Fanning, Johan V. Hultin, and Jeffery K. Taubenberger, "Origin and Evolution of the 1918 "Spanish" Influenza Virus Hemagglutinin Gene." *Proceedings of the National Academy of Sciences USA* 96, no. 4 (1999): 1651–56, DOI: 10.1073/pnas.96.4.1651; Jeremy Brown, *Influenza The Quest to Cure the Deadliest Disease in History* (Melbourne: Text, 2019).
2. Jay P. Graham, John J. Boland, and Ellen Silbergeld, "Growth Promoting Antibiotics in Food Animal Production: An Economic Analysis," *Public Health Reports* 122, no. 1 (2007): 79–87.
3. "Coronavirus Beijing: Why an Outbreak Sparked a Salmon Panic in China," *BBC News*, June 18, 2020, https://www.bbc.com/news/world-asia-china-53089137.
4. "China Suspends Imports of Poultry from Tyson Plant Over COVID-19, Customs Authority Says," *Reuters*, June 21, 2020, https://www.reuters.com/article/us-health-coronavirus-china-tyson-foods/china-suspends-imports-of-poultry-from-tyson-plant-over-covid-19-customs-authority-says-idUSKBN23S0DB.
5. George Lakoff and Mark Johnson, *Metaphors We Live By* (Chicago: Chicago University Press, 1980).
6. Seana Coulson and Vicky T. Lai, "The Metaphorical Brain," *Frontiers in Human Neuroscience* 9 (2016): 699, DOI: 10.3389/fnhum.2015.00699.
7. Petter B. Forsberg and Kristofer Severinsson, "Exploring the Virus Metaphor in Corruption Theory: Corruption as a Virus?" *Ephemera* 15, no. 2 (2015): 453–63.
8. Louis Jakobson, "Are Illegal Immigrants Bringing 'Tremendous' Disease Across the Border, as Trump says? Unlikely," *Polifact.com*, July 23, 2015, https://www.politifact.com/article/2015/jul/23/are-illegal-immigrants-bringing-tremendous-diseas/.
9. Jan Cienski, "Migrants Carry 'Parasites and Protozoa,' Warns Polish Opposition Leader," *Politico.eu*, October 14, 2015, https://www.politico.eu/article/migrants-asylum-poland-kaczynski-election/.
10. "Hungarian Prime Minister Says Migrants Are 'Poison' and 'Not Needed,'" *Guardian*, July 26, 2016, https://www.theguardian.com/world/2016/jul/26/hungarian-prime-minister-viktor-orban-praises-donald-trump.
11. Hugh Raffles, "Mother Nature's Melting Pot," *New York Times*, April 2, 2011, https://www.nytimes.com/2011/04/03/opinion/03Raffles.html.

9. CONTAGIONS

12. Irwin Forseth and Anne Innis, "Kudzu ('Pueraria montana'): History, Physiology, and Ecology Combine to Make a Major Ecosystem Threat," *Critical Reviews in Plant Sciences* 23, no. 5 (2004): 401–13.
13. John Chick, "Invasive Carp in the Mississippi River Basin," *Science* 292, no. 5525 (2001): 2250–51.
14. Barbie Latza Nadeau, "Italy's Olive Trees Didn't Have to Die," *Scientific American*, April 5, 2016, http://www.scientificamerican.com/arti-cle/italy-s-olive-trees-didn-t-have-to-die/.
15. Christy Campbell, *Phylloxera: How Wine Was Saved for the World* (New York: Harper Perennial, 2014).
16. Matteo Ferrari, *Risk Perception, Culture, and Legal Change: A Comparative Study on Food Safety in the Wake of the Mad Cow Crisis* (London: Routledge, 2016).
17. Robert Beach, Fred Kuchler, Ephraim Leibtag, and Chen Zhen, *The Effects of Avian Influenza News on Consumer Purchasing Behavior: A Case Study of Italian Consumers' Retail Purchases*, Economic Research Report no 65 (Washington, DC: USDA, 2008).
18. Eduardo Barberis, "Imprenditori cinesi in Italia. Fra kinship networks e legami territoriali," *Mondi Migranti* 2 (2011): 101–24.
19. Stefano Della Casa, "Le leggende razziste sul cibo cinese (tra coronavirus e non)," *Wired.it*, March 7, 2020. https://www.wired.it/lifestyle/food/2020/03/07/coronavirus-leggende-razziste-cibo-cinese/.
20. Joseph Uscinski, *Conspiracy Theories and the People Who Believe Them* (New York: Oxford University Press, 2019).
21. Ulrich Beck, *Risk Society: Towards a New Modernity* (London: Sage, 1992).
22. Marc van Regenmortel, "The Metaphor That Viruses Are Living Is Alive and Well, but It Is No More Than a Metaphor," *Studies in History and Philosophy of Biological and Biomedical Sciences* 59 (2016): 117–24.
23. Merlin Sheldrake, *Entangled Life: How Fungi Make Our Worlds, Change Our Minds, and Shape Our Futures* (New York: Random House, 2020).
24. Nicole Davis, "Bugs in the System," *Harvard Public Health* (Spring 2017), https://www.hsph.harvard.edu/magazine/magazine_article/bugs-in-the-system/.
25. Joshua Lederberg and Alexa T. McCray, "Ome Sweet 'Omics: A Genealogical Treasury of Words," *Scientist* 15, no. 7 (2001): 8, http://www.the-scientist.com/?articles.view/articleNo/13313/title/-Ome-Sweet—Omics—A-Genealogical-Treasury-of-Words/.
26. Ed Yong, *I Contain Multitudes: The Microbes Within Us and a Grander View of Life* (New York: HarpersCollins, 2016), 3–4.

CONCLUSION

27. Michael Specter, "Germs Are Us," *New Yorker*, October 22, 2012, https://www.newyorker.com/magazine/2012/10/22/germs-are-us.
28. Cindy D. Davis, "The Gut Microbiome and Its Role in Obesity," *Nutrition Today* 51, no. 4 (2016): 167–74; Ching-Hung Tseng and Chun-Ying Wu, "The Gut Microbiome in Obesity," *Journal of the Formosan Medical Association* 118 (2019): S3–S9.
29. Bhagavathi Sundaram Sivamaruthi, Periyanaina Kesika, Natarajan Suganthy, and Chaiyavat Chaiyasut, "A Review on Role of Microbiome in Obesity and Antiobesity Properties of Probiotic Supplements," *BioMed Research International* (2019), https://doi.org/10.1155/2019/3291367.
30. Emily Eaking, "The Excrement Experiment," *New Yorker*, November 24, 2014, https://www.newyorker.com/magazine/2014/12/01/excrement-experiment; A.Vrieze, P. F.de Groot, R. S. Kootte, M. Knaapen, E.van Nood, and M. Nieuwdorp, "Fecal Transplant: A Safe and Sustainable Clinical Therapy for Restoring Intestinal Microbial Balance in Human Disease?" *Best Practice and Research Clinical Gastroenterology* 27, no. 1 (2013): 127–37.
31. Michel Serres, *The Parasite*, trans. Lawrence R. Schehr (Minneapolis: University of Minnesota Press, 2007).

CONCLUSION

1. Elias Canetti, *Crowds and Power* (New York: Noonday, 1984), 219.
2. Canetti, 207.
3. Emil Ludwig, *Colloqui con Mussolini* (Milan: Arnoldo Mondadori, 1970 [1932]), 66.
4. Timothy Snyder, *The Reconstruction of Nations: Poland, Ukraine, Lithuania, Belarus, 1569–1999* (New Haven, CT: Yale University Press, 2004), 174–75.
5. Joel Fetzer, *Public Attitudes Toward Immigration in the Unites States, France, and Germany* (Cambridge: Cambridge University Press, 2000), 151–54.
6. Among many, we can mention Kitchen Connection Alliance (http://18.210.136.33/), League of Kitchens (https://www.leagueofkitchens.com/), and Conflict Kitchen (https://www.conflictkitchen.org/).
7. For example, in 2007, center-left local authorities in Rome tried to introduce ethnic menus in school lunchrooms, causing unexpected and heated reactions not only among politicians but also among parents who felt that foreign food was not nutritious enough or was something their children would not eat. As soon as the right gained control of the administration,

CONCLUSION

the emphasis shifted toward local and regional foods, a strategy that many leftist supporters of local food systems could not oppose. Similar controversies took place in other cities as well. "Dai menù etnici ai menù regionali nelle mense scolastiche romane," *Tuttoscuola*, January 20, 2010, https://www.tuttoscuola.com/dai-men-etnici-ai-men-regionali-nelle-mense-scolastiche-romane/.

INDEX

African Americans, 49–52, 85, 157
agrobiodiversity, 21, 39, 55, 63–64, 83
Ainu, 48
alternative food networks, 57, 66–67
Alternative für Deutschland (German Party), 2
Amazons, 49, 63, 134
antiglobalization, 18, 22, 57, 62, 160, 182
Australia, 59, 147
authenticity, 1, 88–91, 135, 157
authoritarianism, 13, 21

beef, 2, 33, 41–44, 45, 147
Belgium, 145, 149
Belize, 130
Bharatiya Janata Party (Indian Party), 2, 33, 41, 97
Biden, Joe, 45, 173
BJP. *See* Bharatiya Janata Party
Bolsonaro, Jair, 14, 38, 63

Bové, José, 4
boycott, 7, 34, 39, 59, 76
Brazil, 14, 38, 50, 63, 157
British Empire, 59, 98
Buddhism, 43, 46–47

Canada, 7, 61, 99, 148, 165
cannibalism, 36
Caribbean, 36, 50, 61
caste, 17, 41–44
Catalonia, 118–19
chefs, 49–50, 52, 120, 121, 123, 127, 128, 129, 134
China, 40, 48, 78, 103–4, 129, 139, 140–41, 147, 148, 157, 172–74; ancient, 6, 9, 77
class, social, ix, 8, 13, 17, 21, 26, 69, 86, 121
climate change, 13, 38, 40, 45–46
Colombia, 119
colonialism, 98, 116, 122, 125

INDEX

community, 16–17, 35–36, 53, 76, 81–82, 88, 115, 136, 146, 163, 188, 191, 194
Conquistadores, 6, 9
conspiracy theories, 14, 181
cosmopolitanism, 4, 18, 45, 78, 86–87, 124, 132, 158
contagion, 147, 172–186
couscous, 3, 85, 137, 155–56, 170
COVID-19, 92, 10, 100, 147, 149, 172–74, 184, 192
crisis, 14; financial, 10, 98–99

democracy, 12, 14, 21, 29, 37, 189
Denmark, 134
diplomacy, culinary, 7, 128–33, 170
dog meat, 44
Duterte, Rodrigo, 14, 100

ethnicity, 4, 13, 15, 21, 23, 38, 41, 47–53, 150
elites, 4, 12–13, 23, 55, 69, 149, 160, 181
England, 59. *See also* United Kingdom
enslaved people, 49–50, 59, 63, 85
environmental movements, 60–62
Erdoğan, Recep Tayyip, 14, 34
Ethiopia, 40–41, 106
EU. *See* European Union
European Union, 28, 34, 45, 65, 145, 179

fake news, 46, 180–81
famine, 36, 99, 102–4, 178
fast food, 3, 4, 5, 18, 38, 55, 101
food justice, 57, 69, 71
food movement, 23, 57, 67–69, 85, 159, 160, 182

food sovereignty, 4, 23, 57, 69–72, 161, 189
food studies, 19–20
France, 3, 4, 6, 34, 101, 137, 145, 149, 155–56
fungi, 178, 183–84

gastrodiplomacy. *See* diplomacy
gastronationalism. *See* nationalism
gastronativism: definition, 9, 188; exclusionary, 21, 34–53, 124, 133, 141, 147, 151, 158–59, 180, 186, 188, 190, 195; nonexclusionary, 22, 54–72, 124, 133, 156, 159–61, 182, 190
gender, 15, 27; food and, 5, 13, 22, 120–21
Germany, 2, 7, 104, 147, 157
globalization, viii, 10, 12–13, 23, 29, 52, 56–58, 69, 77, 107, 114, 132, 143, 151, 188, 190
GMO, 18, 64–65, 82

halal, 1, 34
heritage, culinary, 81–84, 88, 113, 118, 120, 129, 135–39, 170
Hinduism, 2, 17, 21, 33, 38, 41–43, 86, 98
Hungary, 14, 27, 65

identity, food and, viii, 2, 21, 75–91, 115, 136, 163
ideology, 14; food and, viii, 5, 9, 95
imperialism, 10, 11, 155
Incas, 6
India, 2, 21, 33, 40, 41, 65, 78, 86, 96–98, 121–22, 130

INDEX

indigenous peoples, 26, 36, 48–50, 52, 61, 63, 70, 71, 86
Indonesia, 16, 42, 61
inequality, ix, xiii, 12, 100, 191
intellectual property, 23, 64, 72, 90, 146
Internet, x, 14; of Things, 11, 93, 94, 122, 132
invasive species, 177–78, 182
Islam, 1–3, 17, 27, 33–34, 42, 44, 51, 85, 98, 156
Israel/Palestine, 35, 38–40
Italy, ix, 1–2, 21, 54, 61, 65, 85, 87, 104–6, 111, 117, 144, 157, 179

Japan, 46–47, 48, 59–60, 138, 140, 142–43
Judaism, 17, 26, 36, 169

Kaczyński, Jarosław, 14, 93, 176
kebab, 3, 132, 156–57
kimchi, 129, 138–39, 183

Lega (Italian Party), 3, 5, 38, 85
LGBTQ, 27, 35
local food, 56, 67, 78, 116
locavorism, 67, 194

Macron, Emmanuel, 34
McDonald's, 4, 55–56
meat, 41–47, 85, 96, 149, 157, 165
Mediterranean diet, 57, 137
metaphor, 174–76, 186, 195
Mexico, 50, 64, 79, 120, 137
migrations, ix, 4, 15, 26–27, 71, 123–24, 147, 155–71, 176, 186, 194
minorities, 12, 15, 21, 23, 33, 95, 123, 150, 190, 195

Modi, Nadendra, 2, 14, 97
multiculturality, 1, 15, 86, 124, 158, 160
Muslim. *See* Islam

nation, viii, 6, 8, 16, 22, 37, 115–16, 138, 145
national cuisine, 7, 111–25, 155
nationalism, 116, 147, 150; culinary, 4, 8, 25, 29, 113–17, 127
native Americans, 49, 61
nativism, 25–28, 41, 94
neoliberal globalization. *See* neoliberalism
neoliberalism, 10, 12, 22, 48, 56, 62, 70, 99, 151, 191
Nigeria, 122
Norway, 61, 174
nostalgia, viii, 5, 21, 82, 132

Orban, Viktor, 14, 176
otherness, 13, 15, 17, 27, 29, 35, 53, 76, 194

palm oil, 63
parasite, 180, 186
pastoralism, 40–41
patriotism, ix, 6, 29, 150
Peru, 50, 120, 134
Philippines, 14, 100
pizza, 90, 101, 117, 156, 170
Poland, 14, 21, 44–45, 85, 92, 96, 113, 137, 147, 149, 156, 176
polenta, 3, 38, 85
populism, viii, 14, 28, 147
power, food and, 76, 92–107, 187
Putin, Vladimir, 14

INDEX

race, 13, 21, 27, 45, 47–53, 120, 123, 150
religion, food and, 1, 13, 15, 17, 22, 27, 33, 35, 41, 45
restaurant, 79, 133, 135, 192; ethnic 78, 89, 126, 157, 159, 167–68, 179
Roman empire, 5, 9, 101
Russia, 14, 36, 61, 145, 147

sexual orientation. *See* LGBTQ
Shiva, Vandana, 72
Singapore, 137
slavery. *See* enslaved people
Slow Food, 18, 54–57, 67
socca, 3
social media, 14, 28, 46, 83, 94, 107, 125, 132, 180, 190
South Korea, 129, 138–39
souverainism, x, 28
Soviet Union, 36, 102
Spain, 61, 118, 126–128
sugar, 59, 123, 148
superfoods, 58, 77

Taiwan, 133, 141
technology, 11, 16, 59, 85, 169, 174, 180, 191
Thailand, 87, 128
totalitarianism, 13, 37, 102
tourism, culinary, 78, 83, 133–35, 136
trade wars, 148–52
tradition, culinary, vii, 2, 20, 22, 37, 49, 52, 81–82, 86, 88, 119, 132, 158, 162, 170, 189, 194

transnational corporations, 4, 11, 15, 22, 23, 64, 152, 159
Trump, Donald, 14, 38, 40, 94, 101, 130, 148, 173, 176
Turkey, 14, 34, 145, 170

Uighur, 48, 157
Ukraine, 36, 102, 147
unemployment, ix, 11–12, 26, 159, 172
UNESCO, 83, 135–39, 170
United Kingdom, 7, 15, 124, 130, 149, 178–79
United States, xiii, 6–7, 21, 25, 45, 50, 61, 65, 86, 94, 99–101, 123, 148, 157, 168, 173, 177, 189

Vatican, 1
veganism, 3, 22, 44
vegetarianism, 2, 38, 42, 44
Via Campesina, La, 4, 18, 70–71, 161
Vietnam, 116
virus, 147, 175, 180, 182

West Africa, 85, 116, 122
Western civilization, defense of, 1, 27
whaling, 59–61
Widodo, Joko, 14
WTO, 62, 70, 146, 151

xenophobia, ix, 1, 21, 38, 156, 159

ARTS AND TRADITIONS OF THE TABLE
PERSPECTIVES ON CULINARY HISTORY

Albert Sonnenfeld, Series Editor

Salt: Grain of Life, Pierre Laszlo, translated by Mary Beth Mader
Culture of the Fork, Giovanni Rebora, translated by Albert Sonnenfeld
French Gastronomy: The History and Geography of a Passion, Jean-Robert Pitte, translated by Jody Gladding
Pasta: The Story of a Universal Food, Silvano Serventi and Françoise Sabban, translated by Antony Shugar
Slow Food: The Case for Taste, Carlo Petrini, translated by William McCuaig
Italian Cuisine: A Cultural History, Alberto Capatti and Massimo Montanari, translated by Áine O'Healy
British Food: An Extraordinary Thousand Years of History, Colin Spencer
A Revolution in Eating: How the Quest for Food Shaped America, James E. McWilliams
Sacred Cow, Mad Cow: A History of Food Fears, Madeleine Ferrières, translated by Jody Gladding
Molecular Gastronomy: Exploring the Science of Flavor, Hervé This, translated by M. B. DeBevoise
Food Is Culture, Massimo Montanari, translated by Albert Sonnenfeld
Kitchen Mysteries: Revealing the Science of Cooking, Hervé This, translated by Jody Gladding
Hog and Hominy: Soul Food from Africa to America, Frederick Douglass Opie
Gastropolis: Food and New York City, edited by Annie Hauck-Lawson and Jonathan Deutsch
Building a Meal: From Molecular Gastronomy to Culinary Constructivism, Hervé This, translated by M. B. DeBevoise
Eating History: Thirty Turning Points in the Making of American Cuisine, Andrew F. Smith
The Science of the Oven, Hervé This, translated by Jody Gladding
Pomodoro! A History of the Tomato in Italy, David Gentilcore
Cheese, Pears, and History in a Proverb, Massimo Montanari, translated by Beth Archer Brombert
Food and Faith in Christian Culture, edited by Ken Albala and Trudy Eden
The Kitchen as Laboratory: Reflections on the Science of Food and Cooking, edited by César Vega, Job Ubbink, and Erik van der Linden
Creamy and Crunchy: An Informal History of Peanut Butter, the All-American Food, Jon Krampner

Let the Meatballs Rest: And Other Stories About Food and Culture, Massimo Montanari, translated by Beth Archer Brombert

The Secret Financial Life of Food: From Commodities Markets to Supermarkets, Kara Newman

Drinking History: Fifteen Turning Points in the Making of American Beverages, Andrew F. Smith

Italian Identity in the Kitchen, or Food and the Nation, Massimo Montanari, translated by Beth Archer Brombert

Fashioning Appetite: Restaurants and the Making of Modern Identity, Joanne Finkelstein

The Land of the Five Flavors: A Cultural History of Chinese Cuisine, Thomas O. Höllmann, translated by Karen Margolis

The Insect Cookbook: Food for a Sustainable Planet, Arnold van Huis, Henk van Gurp, and Marcel Dicke, translated by Françoise Takken-Kaminker and Diane Blumenfeld-Schaap

Religion, Food, and Eating in North America, edited by Benjamin E. Zeller, Marie W. Dallam, Reid L. Neilson, and Nora L. Rubel

Umami: Unlocking the Secrets of the Fifth Taste, Ole G. Mouritsen and Klavs Styrbæk, translated by Mariela Johansen and designed by Jonas Drotner Mouritsen

The Winemaker's Hand: Conversations on Talent, Technique, and Terroir, Natalie Berkowitz

Chop Suey, USA: The Story of Chinese Food in America, Yong Chen

Note-by-Note Cooking: The Future of Food, Hervé This, translated by M. B. DeBevoise

Medieval Flavors: Food, Cooking, and the Table, Massimo Montanari, translated by Beth Archer Brombert

Another Person's Poison: A History of Food Allergy, Matthew Smith

Taste as Experience: The Philosophy and Aesthetics of Food, Nicola Perullo

Kosher USA: How Coke Became Kosher and Other Tales of Modern Food, Roger Horowitz

Chow Chop Suey: Food and the Chinese American Journey, Anne Mendelson

Mouthfeel: How Texture Makes Taste, Ole G. Mouritsen and Klavs Styrbæk, translated by Mariela Johansen

Garden Variety: The American Tomato from Corporate to Heirloom, John Hoenig

Cook, Taste, Learn: How the Evolution of Science Transformed the Art of Cooking, Guy Crosby

Meals Matter: A Radical Economics Through Gastronomy, Michael Symons

The Chile Pepper in China: A Cultural Biography, Brian R. Dott

The Terroir of Whiskey: A Distiller's Journey Into the Flavor of Place, Rob Arnold

Epistenology: Wine as Experience, Nicola Perullo

GPSR Authorized Representative: Easy Access System Europe, Mustamäe tee
50, 10621 Tallinn, Estonia, gpsr.requests@easproject.com

www.ingramcontent.com/pod-product-compliance
Lightning Source LLC
Chambersburg PA
CBHW022049290426
44109CB00014B/1040